People of Old Preston

K. A. JOHNSON

WINCKLEY PRESS

This book is dedicated to the memory of my parents
AMELIA and JOHN JOHNSON –
two of the People of Old Preston

Published by Winckley Press
5 Winckley Street
Preston PR1 2AA

ISBN 0-907769-16-0

1994

KEITH ANTHONY JOHNSON

The author is Preston born and was initially educated at St. Augustine's Roman Catholic Boys' School before completing his studies at the Harris College. He is married to Susan and has two young sons, Ethan and Eamon. The family resides in Ingol.

Keith works in the town as an Engineering Designer. He is a keen local historian with a great interest in Preston and its people in the last century. A member of the Lancashire Authors' Association, he had his first work published in 1990.

Both his previous books, "Chilling True Tales of Old Preston" – Books 1 and 2, proved to be local and regional best sellers, being reprinted within three months of publication. The success of these books earned Keith acceptance as a member of the 'Crime Writers' Association'.

ACKNOWLEDGEMENTS

I express my appreciation of the local historians
of a bygone age, particularly

**Peter Whittle,
Anthony Hewitson and
John H. Spencer**

whose accounts of the past are a delight to research.

I also remain indebted to the
**Preston Chronicle,
Preston Guardian,
Preston Pilot,
Preston Herald and
Lancashire Daily Post**
(the forerunner of today's Lancashire Evening Post)

whose dedicated reporters and chroniclers left a legacy of information for the 20th-century historian.

As the **Harris Library and Museum** celebrates its centenary I thank the staff of the Reference Library for their assistance given with such enthusiasm and willingness.

Patricia Crook
My thanks go to Pat who put her literary skills, time and cheerful encouragement at my disposal. I will remain forever grateful.

Glen Crook
My thanks are extended to Glen for his enthusiastic commitment to the book's photographic requirement.

J. C. Fielding
Once again I wish to thank J. C. Fielding for providing line drawings and sketches to appear with Chapters 1,2,6,8,9,11,12, 14,16 and 23.

Outside cover background illustration:
Westall's view of Preston from the North, about 1820

INTRODUCTION

There is, as yet, no time machine to transport us back to those days of old to view a world so far removed from the present age. Although we can return to times long past by studying the lives of those who went before us.

Such is the intention of this book that you and I may journey back to the days when our ancestors occupied the streets of our ancient Borough. Let us therefore take a peep at the people who shaped the town in which we now abide.

Come with me into the time when heroes were not manufactured by the media, but earned their place by human endeavour and achievement.

Tradesman, tailor, spinner, soldier . . . rich man, poor man, clergyman . . . all in their indomitable way contributed to make the lives of Preston's inhabitants interesting and enthralling.

As time passed by, Preston, the winter residence of the gentry, became a town at the very heart of the cotton trade. It meant farewell to the likes of Thomas Winckley as John Horrocks and his contemporaries began to pile brick upon brick to build factories and dwelling places to feed a booming cotton industry.

No doubt the host of cotton barons were inspired by Preston born Richard Arkwright, who had led the way with his eighteenth century spinning frame and his belief in the factory system of production.

Many of them prospered and great multitudes were only too willing to leave their simple country life and flock into the town to sweat all day for shillings. That industry is now in decline but its effects have shaped the very streets in which we live and left a reminder of the workers' daily struggle.

To the setting of industrial growth, with all its attendant necessitities, came people aware of the opportunities that existed. One such man was Matthew Brown, who learnt his father's skill of brewing ale to develop a booming brewery trade, being only too happy to quench the thirst of nineteenth century Preston.

Of course, the folly of the drinker's path was frowned upon by many and the voice of the Temperance Advocates was heard long and hard in those volatile days. From in their midst emerged such men as Joseph Livesey, born in poverty and self taught. History correctly dubbed him the 'Moral Reformer' on account of his tireless endeavours to lead the people of the town along the path of righteousness. His was a righteousness that would lead to proper food, hygiene and clothing.

Meanwhile, the clergy of the town preached from the high ground of the pulpit the need for spiritual food. As humble dwellings increased so did the churches. Traditional places of worship and non-comformist chapels sprung up on Preston's sky line of factories and chimney stacks.

No one had more to do with the growth of churches than the Rev. Carus Wilson who, in a short life span, was responsible for overseeing the construction of a number of places of worship. Some of the places no longer cater for religious needs yet still they stand magnificently proud, a tribute to those who toiled in God's name.

Many who prospered were happy to invest a portion of the wealth earned from Preston's willing workers to improve the town's appearance. No place could ever have had a more generous benefactor than that kindly man, Edmund Robert Harris, who proved the saying "there never was a poor lawyer". Leaving a legacy so grand that we now have a library and museum the envy of many.

Indeed many of the buildings created by those nineteenth century architects remain as testimony to their skill. No mechanical diggers of the modern age were on hand to aid the massive labour employed to construct the monuments. With pick and shovel the labourers of old toiled and grafted to earn a crust or two.

The political scene has always been a volatile one in Preston. The Derby family and the old Borough Council ensuring that only representatives of character and determination could survive our political climate. The Radicals appealed to the masses, but then also did the Stanley household, whose candidates had the backing of the prosperous.

Election time never went unnoticed and was often the signal for rioting and roguery, as candidates clamoured for recognition and the right to represent the townsfolk. Cries such as, 'Down with the tyrant' and, 'Leave not a Freeman alive', heralded the approach of another election.

Despite the wealth of work the underlying poverty was still in place and often the hungry, the angry, the drunk and the ignorant went on the path of lawlessness. For the criminals of the era it meant the dispensing of justice nineteenth-century style. Often they were dispatched to the House of Correction or the reality of life led to the workhouse – a place of fear, dread and revulsion.

Many of course, born within the Borough boundaries, were destined to leave the town and to make their mark upon the world.

Such men were Preston's poetical pair, Francis Thompson and Robert Service. Their styles were different in the extreme yet both produced poetry to make their native town so proud.

Such women were Frances Lady Shelley, the daughter of Thomas Winckley, who became a society lady acquainted with Queen Victoria, and Angela Brazil who, whisked away from Preston as a child, became a writer of esteem with schoolgirl stories of innocent days.

Some fought back from adversity like the cotton outcast John Huntington, whose only crime had been to plead the cause of those oppressed cotton operatives. Yet his departure led to better things and when he returned to town he was a wealthy man.

Some fought for country, proud upon the battlefield. None prouder than the young Thomas Leyland - an English 'Tommy' in the thick of Crimean action, or William Henry Young, a soldier on the Western Front - whose bravery earned a grateful town's gratitude. The many heroes welcomed home helped to erase the pain felt at the loss of the town's sons in battles not so long ago.

Whatever the deed, or whenever the day, I'm sure these tales of local folk are similar to those told of inhabitants of other towns and that they represent the rich tapestry of bygone days.

Whether they were the likes of Preston's 'Grand Old Man' that dedicated doctor Robert Charles Brown, or the humblest mechanic in Joseph Foster's engineering works, they all had a part to play in the Preston of yesteryear, each in many ways dependent upon the other.

So let us remember our proud and vibrant past and enjoy our future in dear old Preston town. I hope that by the time you have read this book you will feel that you have been transported into Preston's distant past and yet in the universe's time, it's really only yesterday.

K A Johnson

The London & Lancashire Fire Insurance Company at about their daily business.

Preston town centre — 1852

CONTENTS

Chapter 1
JOHN HUNTINGTON
'Ten per cent and no surrender'

During the latter part of 1853 and the early part of 1854, Preston was in the throes of a cotton strike, the biggest of many the town had endured over a fifty year period. It became known as the 'Great Strike', or 'Lock Out'and lasted for seven months.

The wages of the operatives had been reduced by 10 per cent in 1842 and a further 10 per cent some five years later. As a consequence in 1853 workers resolved to attempt to regain some of their lost income and have pay level parity at the mills in the town.

The tightly-knit cotton employers branded John Huntington an outcast and he was forced to travel abroad.

The demand was first made by operatives at the Birley Brothers works in Great Hanover Street. The firm opposed the demand; the operatives persisited in the claim and staged a number of strikes.

Fearing a spread of the unrest the general body of employers issued an ultimatum. The dissatisfied hands were told that if they did not resume normal working then the whole of the local establishments would be closed.

The operatives did not return and a general lock out began with over 25,000 workers being thrown out of employment. The action produced much excitement in the public mind, much anger amongst the operatives themselves and a great deal of depression in general trade in the town.

The great cry amongst the operatives was 'Ten per cent and no surrender' and there was great public support for their not unreasonable demand. The action of the Preston employers was denounced near and far and speakers came to lend a sympathetic voice. Ballad-like verses, stating the grievances of the workers and soliciting charity on their behalf, were dolefully sung from town to town, by squalid looking bands of men, women and children.

Week after week, large sums of money were received as collections were made in other northern industrial towns to help them. Despite the assistance from other workers, there was much poverty and suffering in Preston. A cloud of depression seemed to hang over the whole place and every department of trade was in a languid state.

The struggle ended in the defeat of the operatives and they were forced to resume work under the terms of their masters.

With the trade unions then in their infancy, the struggle had been long and bitter and a number of workers' delegates then found it impossible to obtain employment in the local mills. One such delegate was John Huntington, whose services were no longer required at the Ribbleton Lane Factory of Mr. Seed.

Before the lock out he had been a nine shillings a week grinder in the card room of that establishment. In 1852 he had married a young local girl, Jane Beck, who was a weaver at Horrockses' Mill, earning ten shillings per week. They had begun their married life on a joint income of nineteen shillings per week and had set up home in apartments in Ribbleton Lane.

John Huntington went from mill to mill seeking employment but always a shake of the head greeted his request. No local employer would give him employment and soon his meagre savings were used up. He had been branded an outcast by the tightly-knit body of employers and with a young wife and child to support he was in dire straits.

So, in August 1854, the 22-year-old John Huntington went to Liverpool and bargained with the captain of a cargo boat bound for New York, to obtain a working passage at a cost of £3. The boat was set to sail the following day, but the next day he was informed that the sailing had been delayed for a week due to essential repairs being required on the vessel.

With limited means he was unable to wait in Liverpool for a week, so he returned to Preston, much to the surprise of his wife. On the night of his return many friends visited the young couple and, conscious of their desire to face life's struggles together, decided to assist them.

A collection was made amongst their acquaintances and the shillings and half crowns soon mounted up. Within two or three days enough had been raised to pay for the passage of them both and their young infant child.

2

The Huntington family soon collected their belongings and, once again, a much happier John Huntington made his way to Liverpool. When they hurried down to the docks they discovered that the boat had gone. Their despair though was short lived as when the young man explained his plight to another captain of a cargo sailing boat, he consented to take them to New York on the same terms as the former captain.

After being tossed up and down on the ocean for eight weeks, they landed in New York. When they arrived they learned that the boat in which he had planned to sail a week earlier had not arrived. That boat was never heard of again and, later in his life, when John Huntington related that story, he was said to have had tears of gratitude in his eyes.

Once disembarked, the young family had a journey of over 600 miles ahead of them to their intended destination, a farming settlement at Lake Erie, Cleveland. They made the westward journey by railroad and arrived on a very dark night at a log cabin station by the lake side. The night was cold and the wind whistled through the log cabin which was open at both ends, damp, gloomy and fireless, but was their only shelter. Before dawn broke they were overcome by grief as they contemplated their friendless, penniless and hungry condition. Indeed, "had there been a pathway over the Atlantic they would gladly have tramped back to old England barefoot". Between them their only worldly possessions were contained in a green painted box tied with bedcord.

When morning finally arrived John Huntington, a man of unrelenting determination in adversity, sprang to his feet and with one spark of preservation and of hope said to his wife: "Jane, stay here and I will go out and see what I can find". In his wanderings he met a policeman, but he was a foreigner and they could not understand each other.

By and by he came across another policeman who could speak English. This officer directed him to a settlement run by James Wright, a kind-hearted Englishman from Bolton in Lancashire. Following the officer's instructions he arrived at a restaurant owned by the exiled Bolton man and informed him that he too had travelled from Lancashire.

Mr. Wright quizzed his new acquaintance, asking him what there was of note in Preston. John Huntington's reply was: "At the bottom of Church Street there is the House of Correction and I at one time lived just behind it, at No. 2 Henrietta Street". Satisfied with the

The font in St Paul's Church provided by John Huntington

reply, Mr. Wright ordered his servant, Quimbo, a coloured man, to hitch up a wagon and to go with the gentleman to bring his wife, baby and belongings to the settlement.

When they returned there was a hot, substantial meal awaiting them and they were put up for the night. As John Huntington related his bitter experience, Mr. Wright was touched by his story and immediately offered the family shelter whilst they settled in. The new family soon felt welcome and John Huntington's skill as a clock mender and cleaner soon gained him plenty of work. Settlers far and near commissioned his services and they paid him well.

His enthusiasm for work was soon noted and with the help of John Wright he was able to obtain the contract for providing the roof on a new school being built in the area. Other building work followed, including the construction of a couple of wood shanties to house his family and his parents, whom he sent for from their Preston home.

By 1857 he was in business as a contractor, aided by his wife Jane, an educated and accomplished lady. A couple of years later, along with two of his friends a retired colonel and a chemist, he went out for a ramble. As he walked through a field the chemist exclaimed: "What a peculiar smell!" They sniffed about and came to the conclusion that they could smell oil!

They at once sought the owner of the land, an old German settler, who kept pigs and poultry and within days they had bought the holding from him. At once they commenced boring and to their delight they found the land rich in petroleum.

Business began in a small way, but soon improved due to John Huntington's inventiveness in adopting methods for increasing output. What started in that field was to grow into the 'Standard Oil Company', the greatest and wealthiest oil company in the world.

Inevitably, the former Preston factory worker became a millionaire several times over and his name was known worldwide. He became a citizen of the United States of America and was elected a member of the City Council of Cleveland. To both his adopted country and the City that he grew fond of, he was a benefactor.

In 1877, he made a visit to Preston and renewed his acquaintance with some of his former friends and the story of his meteoric rise gladdened the hearts of those who had felt sorrow at his departure.

His next visit was in Guild Year, 1882. On this occasion he arrived with the sad news that his wife had died. Whilst in the town he arranged to supply, at his own expense, a baptistry for St. Paul's Church. Unique in completeness and beauty of decoration, the baptistry was presented in memory of his wife's parents, John and Mary Beck.

A few years after his wife's death he married again, his bride being Marietta Goodwin, the widow of Charles Goodwin. She was a good companion and accompanied him on his travels. These travels included a four year tour of Europe, during which time he was fighting a physical ailment.

While in Europe he had arranged for a magnificent yacht to be built in New York. The cost was enormous but it was to enable him to realise a cherished dream. His heart was set on crossing the Atlantic in his yacht with the star-spangled flag of America flying at the masts, alongside the Union Jack of England. The journey was to end by sailing up the River Ribble into the new dock of his native town.

However, death the great leveller willed it otherwise; he never saw his ship, much less accomplish the purpose on which his heart was set.

He had seemed in high spirits as he began his journey back to America from Europe. Unfortunately, whilst at Southampton he was struck down by pneumonia and quickly passed away.

On that day in January 1893, the wires that lay under the ocean flashed the sad intelligence to America that John Huntington had died in his 61st year. His wife's cablegram told of the intended shipment of his remains by steamer. In an age of superstition the captain and sailors refused to ship the corpse, fearing that the boat may go down in mid-ocean, or be upset by some sea monster.

Eventually, with the aid of the shipping company's directors, some trickery was resorted to. The body was embalmed in London and enclosed in two coffins which were then concealed under rough slabs of timber in a lumber box. The box was placed in the coal bunker and that was the way the millionaire's body was smuggled into New York. On arrival the coffins were stripped of their disguise and his mortal remains conveyed by special train to Cleveland.

He was buried in the Lake View Cemetery, about six miles from the City of Cleveland, close to the mosque of his bosom friend, the martyred President Garfield.

Throughout his life he had been ever mindful of the poor and interested in benevolent enterprises of every kind. It was said that the gifts made during his lifetime exceeded half a million pounds and this generosity led to the construction of the Huntington Art Gallery, Library and Museum in Wade Park, Cleveland.

So ends the story of the man born amidst the working-class terraced homes of Everton Gardens, Preston, who was compelled to sail from Liverpool to New York on a trading vessel, and who now lies surrounded by the illustrious dead of America.

John Huntington – Born 1832 – Died 1893.

Sources:
 'Then and Now' - Pilkington
 'History of Preston' - Hewitson
 'Preston Herald' 10th March 1950.

Chapter 2

EDWARD PEDDER
'As safe as Pedder's Bank'

At the beginning of 1861, one of the most prominent men in Preston was Alderman Edward Pedder. He was the senior partner of the firm of Messrs. Pedder and Co., of the Old Bank in Church Street. An Alderman since 1850, he was a leading figure on the Town Council and was hotly tipped for the position of Guild Mayor in 1862, having spent 17 years as a public representative.

Described as a man of 'unbounded generosity and benevolence', he was highly esteemed by persons of all classes and every shade of opinion, political and religious. An open-handed contributor to every worthy project, he was a magnificent subscriber to countless charities.

The Ashton Park home of Alderman Edward Pedder. His death there in March 1861 led to panic in the town's commercial circles.

The Old Bank in Church Street, Preston

The bank he owned was the first bank opened in Preston. It was situated in Church Street, alongside the Red Lion public house and opposite the Parish Church. When the bank had commenced business in 1776, his grandfather had been in partnership with a Mr. Denison of London. The name of the firm at the outset was Atherton, Greaves and Company, over the years, as the name of the business changed, the name of 'Pedder' was repeatedly in the title.

On Wednesday, 20th March 1861, Edward Pedder carried out his usual daily business affairs and at seven o'clock that evening caught the Ashton omnibus to return to his Ashton Park residence. That night he retired to rest in his apparent usual health.

The following morning he did not make his appearance at the customary hour for breakfast. Concerned at this unusual occurrence, one of the 'domestics' went to his bedroom shortly before nine o'clock and knocked at the door of his chamber. As no answer was returned Mrs. Pedder was informed and she went to the room and found her husband in convulsions.

A messenger was at once despatched for Mr. Hall the surgeon who immediately hastened to Mr. Pedder's assistance. Unfortunately, the banker was beyond medical aid, for after Mr. Hall's arrival he breathed only two or three times before expiring, the cause of death being 'apoplexy'.

Banker Edward Pedder

The town was stunned when news spread of the death of the banker, councillor and magistrate, who was only in his 51st year. He had been married since October 1834 to Amelia, and was the father of two sons and three daughters. Born in a house in Fishergate he was the eldest son of Mr. James Pedder, and had three brothers and four sisters.

One of his brothers was Major H. N. Pedder of the 11th (Preston) Volunteer Rifles and a partner in the bank; another was Captain C.D. Pedder of the 39th Regiment and the third was Captain Thomas Pedder of the 7th Hussars, who died in India of sunstroke during the mutiny there.

Following closely upon the sudden death of Edward Pedder, the Preston public received a massive shock on 10th April, 1861 when a notice was posted on the door of the bank. It simply read: 'IN CONSEQUENCE OF THE DEATH OF THE LATE MR. EDWARD PEDDER, THE BANK IS CLOSED, AND THE BUSINESS WILL BE WOUND UP'.

It is impossible to describe the consternation which this brief notification caused throughout the town. The news spread with great rapidity and was the main topic of conversation in all circles. Crowds of people went to the bank with the sole purpose of reading the announcement for themselves.

There was a great feeling of sorrow that an establishment that had long been a credit to the town, and had been run by such eminent people, had collapsed. Following the announcement of the death of Mr. Pedder there had been a continual drain on the banks resources and a general feeling of uneasiness in commercial circles.

Henry Newsham Pedder, the brother and partner of the deceased, was forced to make the decision to close the doors of the establishment. In a letter to the creditors he explained the situation and expressed the hope that when the accounts had been addressed there would be sufficient monies to ensure that no serious deficiences would occur. Although a partner in the bank he had never taken any part in the management of affairs during his brother's time.

Immediatley the news of the collapse of the Old Bank was revealed, Henry Newsham Pedder resigned his commission as Major of the 11th Lancashire (Preston) Rifle Volunteer Corps, in order to channel his energies to the sorting out of his brother's affairs.

With the aid of a firm of accountants the staff of the bank set about the task of balancing the books in order to present them to the creditors. In all, the creditors numbered more than 4,000 a large proporiton of which were for small amounts, with the largest not exceeding £12,000.

On the Monday following the closure, the bank was opened for the reception of holders of deposit receipts whose surname began with the letters 'A' to 'C' inclusive. This led to a tremendous rush to the doors and the clerks had not a moments respite during the whole day. Many scores of receipt holders, whose surnames began with every letter of the alphabet, presented their receipts. Although in contravention of the advertisement in the previous Saturday's paper, they were dealt with to prevent the necessity of a second visit. Consequently on later days the visitors were much less.

Eventually the aggregate of dividends paid to the depositors was 17s.6d. in the pound.

The building, which was erected in 1690, continued as a bank with a branch of the Manchester and County Bank opening there in 1862. To this day the site of the Old Bank is occupied by one of the town's leading banks.

Edward Pedder born 10th August 1810 - died 21st March 1861.

Postscript:
As long ago as 1792 'Pedder's' had been the only bank in Preston. Around that time there was a monetary crisis in England and about 300 of the country's banks stopped payment. Pedder's Bank was one of only 50 in the whole country that stood its ground. Consequently in those days the common saying in Preston and district was, 'As safe as Pedder's'.

Sources:
  'Preston Guardian' 23rd March 1861
  'Preston Chronicle' April 1861
  Hewitson's History of Preston. P238

Chapter 3

THOMAS DUCKETT & SON

A Loss Not Easily Replaced

On Whit Monday, 1852, a day observed as a general holiday, a vast multitude numbering many thousands gathered in Winckley Square and the Cross Street area of Preston. The reason for the public attendance was the inauguration of the statue dedicated to Sir Robert Peel, the former Prime Minister of Great Britain. An unfortunate accident had cut short his life in 1850, at the age of 62, when he had fallen from his horse while out riding. The inhabitants of Preston, as those of other towns, showed their appreciation of the man by subscribing to a suitable monument. The great act of his political life had been the abolition of the Corn Laws, an act which had enshrined his memory in the hearts of a grateful people.

The task of executing a statue of the departed statesman was entrusted to Thomas Duckett, Senior, a well known and respected Preston sculptor. The model was commenced in December, 1850 the material selected for the statue being a durable species of limestone obtained from a quarry on the Borwick estate in the County of Lancashire.

Thomas Duckett, a native of Preston, took great delight in creating the magnificent monument. Having been apprenticed to the trade of a plasterer he had left the town to seek work, firstly as a wood carver in Lancaster and then as a marble worker and sculptor in Liverpool; an occupation that was to lead him onto Kendal to one of the most reputable marble works in the Kingdom.

At ease with mallet and chisels, he returned to his native town in the early 1840s and took a dwelling house and premises in Cannon Street, prior to establishing a studio in Avenham Road, from where he became known as a 'portrait sculptor of the most respectable rank'.

The unveiling ceremony on that Whit Monday morning was carried out by the Mayor of Preston, Alderman Thomas Monk, and the immense assembly was most impressed when the work of art was revealed.

Amongst those admiring the sculptor's work that day was his son, Thomas Duckett, Junior, who was keen to follow in his father's footsteps. Born in Kendal in 1839, shortly before his family returned to Preston, the young Duckett was later sent by his father to study at the Royal Academy in London. The purity and refinement of his models soon brought him into the notice of some of the leading sculptors of the period.

With a view to ripening his knowledge he, along with his young wife, Lizzie, went to Rome. They spent two years amongst the vast treasures of art contained in the 'Eternal City' before returning to London accompanied by their baby daughter, Lucy, born while they were abroad.

Towards the end of his stay in Italy the young sculptor had been troubled by a hacking cough and chest pains and his return to these shores did nothing to improve his health. Seeking medical advice he was informed that he was suffering from consumption/pulmonary tuberculosis as it was known in those days.

The distressed young man found that the disease was developing to such an extent that he was forced to seek a more favourable climate. Acting on medical advice, in March 1866 he boarded a cargo vessel bound for the shores of Australia, and his wife and young child waved him goodbye from the quayside.

His first stop was Melbourne, Victoria, where he found several friends. He spent some months there in the hope of regaining his shattered health. Sadly the climate proved to him, as to other consumptive patients, highly unfavourable on account of the extreme and sudden variableness in the temperature.

SIR
ROBERT PEEL.
BARONET

ERECTED
BY PUBLIC SUBSCRIPTION
1852

On Whit Monday, 1852 a vast multitude gathered in Winckley Square to witness the unveiling of the Peel statue.

12

Acting on sound advice, he tried other portions of the Australian continent and had a short stint in Tasmania, the 'Garden of the Southern Seas'. Eventually, in July 1867, he proceeded to Sydney, where the climate appeared to be more congenial to his condition. As a result, he was able to follow his professional pursuits, and a bust of the then Governor of New South Wales, John Young, and several paintings for the visit of the Duke of Edinburgh helped to enhance his reputation. The young sculptor was soon inundated with commissions but unfortunately he found himself unable to execute them owing to the ravages of his complaint.

Ironically, among his last and most impressive works were four colossal angels for Haslam Creek Cemetery. The figures represented Death, Mercy and the Resurrection and were in position only a few short weeks before a hearse carrying the body of the young sculptor entered the same cemetery.

His death on the last Sunday in April, 1868 at the age of 29, came six months after he had received news from home of his wife's premature death in Wolverhampton. With his own failing health, he felt unable to do anything but leave his daughter and a son he had never seen, to the care of relatives in Preston.

Meanwhile Thomas Duckett, Senior's, work continued to be admired in Preston and he was still occupying his no. 45 Avenham Road studios in February, 1878, when he died aged 74, after an illness of considerable duration. One of the last public works executed by him was the beautiful marble altar at St. Augustine's Church in Frenchwood.

Twice married Thomas, Senior, had by his first wife one son named Richard, who eventually followed a vocation in the church. Richard spent many years in Portugal before ending his days as a Canon in Norwich.

By his second wife he had two sons and two daughters. All of them developed artistic skills none more so than their eldest son Thomas Duckett, Junior, in whose death the world sustained a loss not easily replaced.

Thomas Duckett, Senior's, death was announced with the headline, 'Death of a Celebrity'. He is buried in Preston Cemetery. On one side of his gravestone is a likeness of himself and on the reverse side are the sculptured features of his second wife Winifred. The inscriptions reveal the death of his wife three years earlier and the death of their beloved grand-daughter, Lucy, aged 13, shortly before his own passing. In his last resting place Thomas Duckett, Senior, is surrounded by many impressive sculptures, a number of which are the result of his talented labours.

The Peel statue in Winckley Square still remains as a constant reminder of the immense skill of the Duckett family of 19th-century Preston. Sadly, the name of Alderman Thomas Monk, who unveiled the statue and whose name appeared on the plinth, was officially removed with a chisel, following his trial at Lancaster Assizes for the forgery of a Will.

Sources:
   'Preston Chronicle' 1852
   'Preston Guardian' June 1868
   'Preston Guardian' February 1878

Thomas Duckett, Senior, an admired sculptor, died in February 1878. His gravestone in Preston Cemetery carries a likeness of himself and his second wife Winifred. He lies surrounded by many impressive sculptures - many the result of his talented labours.

Chapter 4

JOSEPH FOSTER & SONS
Praise Heaped Upon The Town's Mechanics

As long ago as 1744, Preston's first newspaper appeared on the streets, it was called the 'Preston Journal'. It had only a short existence, as did the 'True British Courant', which was published the following year.

A more serious attempt at establishing a regular newspaper was made in 1791 with the commencement of the 'Preston Review', which managed to survive for about twelve months. It was not until the 19th century that publishers managed to produce newspapers with any continuity. 'The Journal' arrived on the scene in 1807 and this became the cornerstone of the 'Preston Chronicle' with which it merged in 1812.

Lawrence Dobson was the man behind the 'Preston Chronicle' and his rival in the newspaper stakes became Lawrence Clarke, who published firstly, in 1821, the 'Preston Sentinel', which survived a year, and secondly, the 'Preston Pilot', in 1825 which was to have much greater longevity. Briefly opposition arrived from the 'Preston Observer' and the 'Preston Advertiser', but it was not until 1844 when Joseph Livesey established the 'Preston Guardian', that serious competition arrived.

Other newspapers that appeared on the scene to tempt those who could read included the 'Preston Mercury', 'Preston Observer', 'The Echo', 'Preston Telegraph', 'The Wasp' and the 'Preston Herald'. The latter became, like the 'Preston Chronicle' and 'Preston Guardian', well establised as a weekly, supplemented by mid-weekly issues. These papers attempted to establish daily publications but their initial attempts were soon abandoned.

With the industry gradually gaining momentum there was cause for celebration throughout the town in December, 1872. The first Saturday of that month saw the first newspapers roll off the new 'Web' printing machine at the 'Preston Guardian' . The machine had been produced in Preston by local inventive and constructive skills. The machine was the creation of Walter Bond, the foreman of the newspaper and Joseph Foster who had constructed the press at his Iron Works in St. Paul's Square.

A year earlier the proprietor of the 'London Times' had begun to print that journal on a new machine which had been invented and built, in the utmost secrecy, on their premises. The Bond and Foster Press was said to be a significant advance on the 'London Times' press and it was appropriately named 'The Prestonian'. Both these presses were successful in printing from a reel of paper, some miles in length, thus dispensing with manual feeding of flat sheets, which was a very labour-intensive process, requiring eight people to feed the sheets in and eight more to take them out.

James Yates Foster, son of the founder, ensured his father's enterprise continued

The machine was necessary to respond to the great increase in newspaper circulation following the repeal of Newspaper Stamp Duty and the Duty on paper.

'The Prestonian' was the forerunner of the huge machines used in the newspaper offices of today. The mechanics of the town had praise heaped upon them and it was a significant stage in the life of Joseph Foster who, in 1860, at the age of 29 had commenced manufacture in Avenham Street, Preston, of machines for rapidly folding newspapers.

Born in Foster's Square in May, 1831 he was at a tender age apprenticed to Messrs. Ainscough and Tomlinson, progressing to foreman by the time he was 19. After serving his time, he acquired experience at various works before beginning work on his own account.

Following the success of 'The Prestonian' Joseph Foster went on from strength to strength and in the following years purchased the Peel Hall Foundry and built the Bow Lane Ironworks. In the year 1882, his two sons, Frank and James Yates Foster were taken into partnership and further expansion led to the purchasing of offices in

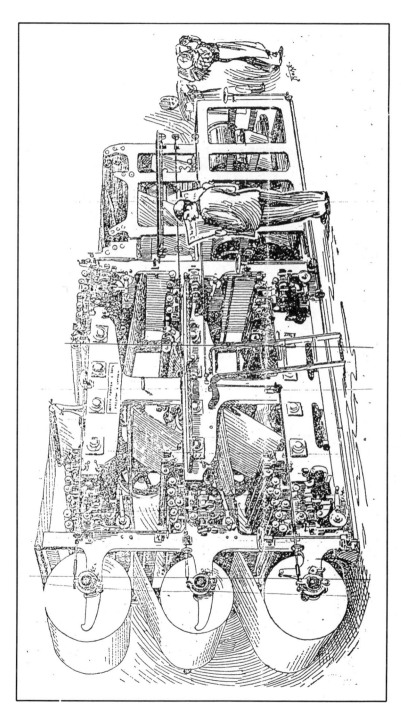

The 'Three-decker' printing press supplied to the Preston Guardian by Preston company, Joseph Foster & Sons.

London, including one in Fleet Street, at the very hub of the newspaper world.

Once again, in June, 1898, the Foster family hit the headlines when the 'Preston Guardian' proudly announced that production had commenced on their new 'three-decker' printing machine supplied by Preston's much acclaimed press manufacturer.

In the early days papers did not appear with more than eight pages and the newspaper was proud to announce that the 'Preston Guardian' could, without the necessity of hand inserted sections, produce 12 pages at 'one pass' and was capable of up to 24 pages, should the necessity arise. With reels of 11 miles of continuous paper, the press was capable of producing a 6 page newspaper at the rate of 50,000 copies per hour.

Beside the 'Preston Guardian', which had survived to be the town's leading weekly, the press was also used to print the 'Lancashire Daily Post', the forerunner of the present day 'Lancashire Evening Post'. The first edition of the 'Lancashire Daily Post' printed on the machine, was an eight page, six column paper which carried a full report of the death of former Prime Minister Mr. Gladstone.

Frank Foster for many years became the mainstay of the engineering business and the family were dealt a severe blow in the year 1900, when he died. His father immediately looked to his younger son James Yates Foster to handle affairs and he took up the challenge with great determination. He was a busy man involved in both business and political affairs, in fact the new century heralded him as Mayor of Preston.

When Joseph Foster passed away in August 1913, aged 82, James Yates Foster became the sole proprietor of the firm. In 1922 he followed the example of his father by admitting his two sons, Major John Hendry Foster and Mr. Frank Foster into partnership with him.

On the occasion of James Yates Foster's 70th birthday, a dinner was held at the Public Hall to honour a man who had served as an Alderman, Justice of the Peace and Lt. Colonel with the Territorial Artillery. It was attended by civic dignatories, business friends and all the company's employees. At the event in July, 1925 Lt. Colonel Foster spoke of the great advances that had been made since the firm's founding in 1860. He recalled the days when there were no electric cranes and very few hand cranes, no milling machines or such aids to labour. The working week was 60 hours and a skilled man's pay was 26s. a week. He also mentioned the time when the workmen accepted a pay cut to help his father through a difficult period.

While the Foster family had been busy with innovating designs in Preston, in America two brothers, Fred and Sam Goss were making similar advances. In 1855 they began the developing of printing presses in that country and in the early part of the 20th century the Goss Company established a factory in Middlesex. The British, Continentals and Scandinavians were their targets and in January, 1936, the Joseph Foster Company, then in the hands of his grandsons, was acquired by the American Company.

The business founded by the Foster family has survived in the town, despite the usual takeovers and name changes and is at present part of the extensive North American Rockwell Corporation trading under the title Rockwell Graphic Systems. Part of a multi-national organisation, it still owes much to the enterprise and engineering skills of the Foster family in those formative years.

Joseph Foster – Born 4th May 1831 – Died August 1913, 82 years old.

Postscript:

In Guild year 1882, the people of Preston had the following regular publications at their disposal:

'Preston Chronicle', every Saturday, price 2d.

'Preston Guardian', every Wednesday, price 1d. every Saturday price 2d.

'Preston Herald', every Wednesday, price 1d. every Saturday price 2d.

'Preston Pilot' every Wednesday, price 1½d.

Sources:
Hewitson's History of Preston p.341
'Preston Guardian' 14.12.1872
'Preston Guardian' 4.6.1898
'Preston Guardian' 16.8.1913
'Preston Gaurdian' 1.8.1925

Chapter 5

MATTHEW BROWN
Strong Brew at a Penny a Pint

MR. JOSEPH BROWN.

MR. JOS. SMITH.

Matthew Brown died in 1883 leaving behind a thriving company. His son Joseph Brown failed to get re-elected to the board in 1880, but son-in-law Joseph Smith ensured the family link was maintained.

In 1830, with the Industrial Revolution in full swing, the Government introduced legislation for the abolition of Beer Duty. This act gave everyone the freedom to retail beer for an annual payment of a two guinea registration charge. It was aimed at removing the seamy gin palaces that had sprung up following the introduction of Beer Duty.

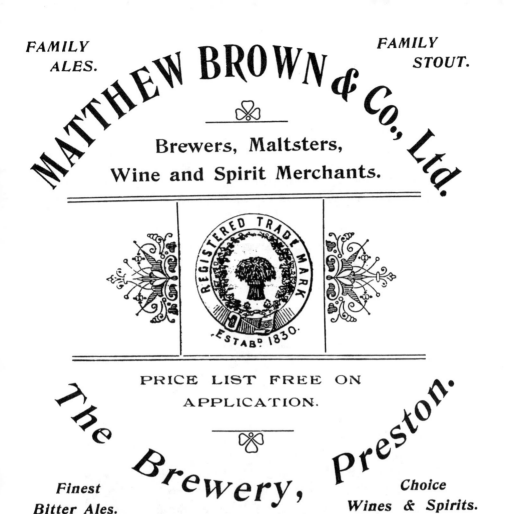

Strong brew at a penny a pint from Matthew Brown's brewery.

The population of towns, including Preston, was rising at an explosive rate with mills being erected together with dense housing areas. For the mass of working people there was only the public houses to provide relief from their day-to-day existence. Solace was cheap and easy to find, with strong beer costing only a penny a pint and the pubs remaining open for up to 20 hours a day.

The circumstances were ideal for a young and energetic man by the name of Matthew Brown who, based at a shop in Pole Street, took the opportunity of developing a brewing business of great significance. The shop had been built by his father about 1824, and following

21

his father's death, Matthew Brown commenced brewing and gradually extended the premises. Next, he purchased an old stone yard and erected what was later known as the Anglers' Inn, moving there and retaining the old premises for brewing purposes only. The inn was situated at the corner of Pole Street and Lords Walk, not far from the site of his original beerhouse, which was eventually developed into the Pole Street Brewery.

In 1840 nearly 30,000 publicans nationwide brewed their own beer, but this age-old tradition came under attack as the brewery companies set out to establish chains of their own public houses, and so develop the tied system. During the following 30 years Matthew Brown went a long way towards creating the nucleus of his empire in Preston. He bought houses, built others, lent money to some and, in many cases, he traded with publicans alongside their own home brews.

The main brewery and offices of Matthew Brown were situated at the junction of Pole Street and Percy Street.

By 1875 he had built the business up into a healthy concern, making a steady profit of £8,000 a year, and at this stage he converted the business into a limited liability company. He handed a 10 per cent shareholding to each of his two sons and sold the remaining 80 per cent share to the public.

Matthew Brown's intention was to set up the company and then retire leaving the management of affairs to his sons, and this he did. However by 1879, he was recalled to the Board as other directors came and went. Even his son Joseph failed to get himself re-elected in 1880 and as his second son Richard had died, Matthew Brown was the only family link with the past.

Fortunately before he died in 1883, aged 76, he had the satisfaction of knowing that the family association with the company was being maintained through the endeavours of his son-in-law, Joseph Smith, a prominent cotton manufacturer in Preston. At the time of the founder's passing, the company had registered offices and a brewery in Pole Street and Percy Street, malthouses in Lark Hill, Maudland, Moor Park and Lawson Street, 20 properties with a full licence, 26 with a beer licence, 4 off-licences, 24 leased premises and 40 premises whose custom was secured by loans.

Besides his endeavours in the brewery trade Matthew Brown was also a very enthusiastic farmer and breeder of cattle and sheep. From childhood he had been taught farming ways, having been born on a small Samlesbury farm in 1807 and later having moved with his family to another farm in the Ribbleton area of Preston.

For many years he looked after hundreds of acres of land at Whitewell which belonged to the Towneley family. Indeed, at a public dinner some time before his death he received from Colonel Towneley a handsome and costly solid silver centre piece in recognition of the service he had rendered to agriculture in that part of the country. He was a prominent figure at the leading shows and on numerous occasions he was among the prize winners.

Matthew Brown's firm became famous for their special brand of beer known as 'Old Tom', which was supplied to many inns and taverns in the town. Many of the pubs displayed a cardboard advertisement showing the face of a cat, highly coloured, with sly wide open eyes and thick strong whiskers with the slogan underneath 'Try our Old Tom' and many did and went back for more.

The Anglers' Inn, where Matthew Brown lived until 1860, always retained a place in his affection and every year he insisted that the statutory annual meetings were held there. In those early days it

The Anglers' Inn at the corner of Pole Street and Lord's Walk always retained a place in Matthew Brown's affection. The inn was demolished in August 1968.

was a well known meeting place of various trade societies of the town and was famous for its catering.

The inn's chief characteristic was the large sculptured figure over the doorway. This depicted an angler in the act of fishing. He was wearing the quaint costume of the mid 19th century which included his semi-tall hat, his fishing basket was over his shoulder and in his right hand he held a fishing net. In the other hand was the rod complete with line, held aloft. The whole composition was a delicate and attractive work of art and the angler represented was believed to have been a friend of Matthew Brown.

Eventually, in August 1968, time caught up with this old established inn and the demolition workers moved in. It was farewell to a public house steeped in memories of the early days of Matthew Brown brewing.

Following the death of Matthew Brown, steady but unspectacular progress followed for the company and, despite the intervention of the war years, they succeeeded in the take-overs of a number of breweries in the region. It was in 1927 however that the most significant development came. A move to Blackburn followed the acquisition of the Lion Brewery at Little Harwood. A switch in policy meant the use of the Lion trademark and to the drinking man the red, rampant lion was the sign that greeted them.

In recent times the company has been taken over by Scottish and Newcastle and the parent company have announced plans to cease brewing at the Blackburn brewery.

Despite all the mergers and take-overs the name Matthew Brown still looms large in Preston. There are still close on 150 public houses in the town and over a quarter of them carry the name of the man who took advantage of the abolition of Beer Duty to build a brewing business. He is remembered as a self-made man, a true 'John Bull' type character.

Matthew Brown, Born 1807 - Died January 1883 – aged 76 years.

Sources:
'Preston Illustrated'
'Preston Guardian'
January 1883

Amidst the gravestones in Preston Cemetery is the imposing family vault in which Matthew Brown was laid to rest.

Chapter 6

Mrs Livesey   *Joseph Livesey*

JOSEPH LIVESEY
"Thee Sign First"

While Matthew Brown was taking advantage of the Government's abolition of Beer Duty in 1830 at his brewery in Pole Street, Preston, another local man, Joseph Livesey was at work striving to come to terms with the painful poverty and dark despair that was rampant in Preston and throughout the country.

Living standards were generally at a sub-human level. The Corn Laws were at the root of the evil, keeping bread prices cruelly high. For many the gin parlour, beer shop and public house were the only places of refuge from the cruelties of life.

Joseph Livesey tackled the effects by preaching a new morality and pleading with the apathetic to abandon the use of ale, porter, wine, arden spirits and all intoxicating liquors except as medicine.

Born on 5th March, 1794 at Walton-le-Dale, Joseph Livesey had survived a tough upbringing, having lost both his parents within the space of 10 weeks when only seven years old. In the care of his grandfather and uncle, he spent a laborious youth, firstly winding

John King, one of the 'Seven men of Preston' - 'Thee sign first' - urged Joseph Livesey.

weaving bobbins and then as soon as he was able, following the occupation of a weaver. He laboured for seven years in a damp dismal cellar and with what little leisure time he had, he pursued his studies amid the same cheerless surroundings. From these beginnings developed a man who was possessed of a great sense-of-humour and who became a popular leader, ever aware of the suffering of his fellow human beings.

Up to the year 1831, when he was 37 years of age he was what might be called a moderate drinker, or to put it more definitely, his indulgence in alcoholic liquor was limited to 'a glass or two when travelling' and 'a glass or two on market day'.

By then he was the proprietor of a cheese shop at 28 Church Street and a familiar figure with his market stall and his tireless efforts conducting adult education classes in Cannon Street.

On the first day of 1832, a teacher of the school established a Temperance Society. The pledge then adopted was what soon became known as one of 'moderation', for the facts of it allowed those who signed it the use of fermented liquors in moderation with total abstinence from distilled liquors.

While pleased with the progress made, Joseph Livesey did not feel this pledge went far enough and, following discussions at his place of business in Church Street with another Waltonian, John King, he drew up another pledge that advocated 'Total Abstinence', as opposed to 'Moderation'.

On August 23rd, 1832 Joseph Livesey had partaken of his last glass of whisky. "Thee sign first", he urged John King and he did so, with Joseph Livesey then adding his signature.

The first step led to the next, for in the course of a few days notice of a Special Meeting was given, to be held in the Temperance Hall (the Old Cockpit) on the next-but-one Saturday night, September 1st,

1832. The subject was warmly discussed and at the close of the meeting a group gathered together and signed the new pledge. The seven signatories who endorsed the Temperance Pledge, became known as the 'Seven Men of Preston', and their names were inscribed in an old memorandum book belonging to Joseph Livesey. With the meeting being held on a Saturday night many of the leading Temperance advocates were unable to attend. As a result the signatures of many of the movement's most enthusiastic followers were missing from the original pledge.

A great movement had been born and through the cities of England Joseph Livesey preached his beliefs and from inspired audiences came countless converts. The Old Cockpit became the hub of Preston's Temperance movement and large crowds gathered every Tuesday evening to hear a long list of speakers who extolled the virtues of giving up the 'demon drink'.

Many of the speakers had been intemperant and one of them, Thomas Swindlehurst, was proud to be known as the 'King of the Reformed Drunkards'. Perhaps the most brilliant orator of the day was Edward Grubb, while Henry Anderton became affectionately known as the Temperance Poet of the period.

Joseph Livesey's Cheese Shop in Church Street.

Discussing the pledge with John King.

The following is an exact facsimile of the first pledge - drawn up by Mr Livesey, on the 1st September 1832:

We agree to Abstain from All Liquors of an Intoxicating Quality, whether Ale Porter Wine, or Ardent Spirits, except as Medicine.

John Gratrix
Edw° Dickinson
Jno: Broadbelt
Jno: Smith
Joseph Livesey
David Anderton.
Jno: King.

By the end of 1834, Preston had almost 4,000 teetotallers and Joseph Livesey was understandably delighted. His lecture on 'Malt Liquor' delivered in 1832, was a great inspiration for the movement, whose origins in a diluted form began in America in the late 18th Century.

Not satisfied with his contribution to the well-being of society, Joseph Livesey decided in 1842 to begin the production of a halfpenny weekly paper entitled 'The Struggle'. His compassion for the working classes knew no bounds and his regard for politicians was non-existent. As a result the paper sought to right wrongs and bring them to the notice of all who would read them. Week after week he gave eye witness accounts of the poverty and degradation that abounded. The hungry children, the homeless families, the poor widow, all had their stories told in the publication that ran for four years. 'Repeal the Corn Laws' screamed the paper's headlines as politicians remained stubbornly ignorant of the wretchedness prevailing.

The Temperance Movement was no short term solution to the problems of society, but gradually it had its effect on the way people viewed the dangers of drunkenness. While Joseph Livesey's premises in Church Street were the centre of the movement, by 1850 there were three Temperance Hotels in Preston; in Cannon Street, Lune Street and Fishergate. In 1878 an enterprise under the banner 'Preston Coffee Tavern Company' was launched with premises in Friargate, named 'Queens' and in Church Street named 'Alexandra's'. The aim was to provide coffee and cocoa drinks all day, including early morning, for the benefit of people going to work. Despite the enthusiasm of the originators the so-called 'Taverns' never really took off and within a few years the enterprise was dissolved.

In 1882, exactly 50 years after the signing of the pledge, a national celebration was held at the Crystal Palace and it was attended by 50,000 people. Alive to celebrate the occasion was Joseph Livesey and he received many tributes to his unselfish work, being acknowledged as the one who planted the Teetotal standard in London and the great provincial towns of Birmingham, Leeds, Bradford, Darlington, New-castle and Sunderland.

He died two years later, in September, 1884 at his Preston residence of 13 Bank Parade, where he had lived since 1856. He received glowing obituaries in all the newspapers of the day including 'The Times', which acknowledged his great contribution to the welfare of his fellow man.

Joseph Livesey had been a thrifty and prosperous tradesman, who declared that his wife had been, "The greatest blessing of my life". He was very proud of his large family having altogether nine sons and four daughters, although four of them, like so many in those days, died in infancy. As the years progressed his eldest sons became of great assistance to him, in both his cheese business and his printing and

In 1832 in the Cockpit, Joseph Livesey delivered his famous lecture on the perils of malt whisky.

IN AFFECTIONATE REMEMBRANCE
OF
JOSEPH LIVESEY,
OF PRESTON,
WHO DIED SEPTEMBER 2ND, 1884,
IN THE 91ST, YEAR OF HIS AGE,
AFTER AN HONOURED LIFE OF PHILANTHROPY
AND USEFULNESS, AS AUTHOR AND WORKER,
AS THE PIONEER OF TEMPERANCE, THE ADVOCATE
OF MORAL AND SOCIAL REFORM, AND THE HELPFUL
FRIEND AND COUNSELLOR OF THE POOR.

*The grave of Joseph
Livesey in Preston
Cemetery with a
close-up of the
inscription on top*

publishing activities. One of his most significant achievements in the printing world was the starting of the 'Preston Guardian' in February, 1844, which was first published from his Church Street premises. Helped in the production by three of his sons, he eventually sold the paper to George Toulmin, founder of the 'Lancashire Evening Post' in 1859.

Joseph Livesey's funeral was a great one in a representative sense with persons present from all parts of the kingdom. As the funeral cortege made its way to Preston Cemetery all the shutters and blinds were drawn en route, including those of public houses, and dram-shops. A scroll on top of his grave records his honoured life with the words 'The helpful friend and counsellor of the poor'.

Joseph Livesey – Born 5th March 1794 – Died September 1884.

Postscript:

Joseph Livesey's benevolent attitude was shown in 1858 when drinking fountains were fixed in Fishergate, Church Street, Lune Street, North Road, Lancaster Road and Bridge Lane, at his expense. The Corporation followed his generous action by placing a number of fountains in other parts of the Borough. In 1871 a somewhat elaborate drinking fountain, made of white marble, red granite and freestone, was erected in Lancaster Road. This fountain carried the following inscription:-

'Jesus said, whosoever drinketh of this water shall thirst again; but whosoever drinketh of the water that I shall give him shall never thirst. John IV., 13'.

In the winter of 1881 the water with which this fountain was supplied was shut off, owing to the annoying way mischievous children played with it.

Sources:
Autobiography of Joseph Livesey.
Story of Joseph Livesey's Life, by John Weston, 1884.
'Preston Guardian', June 1907.

Chapter 7

RICHARD 'DICKY' TURNER
"Nothing But Tee-Total Will Do"

One Thursday evening in October, 1832 Richard 'Dicky' Turner, after paying his customary daily visit to one of Preston's ale houses, set off in the general direction of home. As he walked the streets of the town his attention was drawn to St. Peter's schoolroom where a gathering of local people were holding one of their regular Temperance Meetings.

More drunk than sober he entered the schoolroom intent on a little fun. However, the words that spilled from the lips of the dedicated orators had a profound effect on the intemperate observer and, by the time the meeting was over, he had been converted to the flock. Without more ado he added his name to the pledge and committed himself to abstaining from all intoxicating liquors for a week.

It was a significant moment for Richard Turner the 42 year old fish hawker, who was born at Bilsborough, near Preston on 20th July, 1790. His parents had moved to Preston when he was a mere boy and he had been sent to work in a cotton factory. Later apprenticed as a plasterer he eventually forsook that occupation to sell fish in Preston's streets. A familiar figure in the town, he managed to earn enough money to support a wife, whom he had married at 28, and two daughters, as well as take his daily tipple.

Full of enthusiasm for his new found cause he frequently addressed the weekly audiences at the Old Cockpit. It was during one of those stuttering speeches that he blurted out the phrase, "Nothing but the tee-total would do." The phrase had a captivating effect on the audience who loudly cheered as Joseph Livesey, the father of the Temperance Movement, patted him on the back and said, "That shall be the name, Dicky". From that meeting in 1833, came the word Teetotal which was to become the byword of the Temperance Movement. The word can now be found in all English and American dictionaries and is described as meaning abstinence from intoxicating liquors.

His initial week-long commitment to abstinence was to turn into a lifelong one and his zeal and passion were irresistible. This man of medium stature, with a dark ruddy complexion and full earnest eyes, would tour the streets sporting a white hat and, with the aid of a watchman's rattle, would alert the neighbourhood to the imminent Temperence Meeting, due to be held in that area.

Such was the enthusiasm of this disciple of the movement that at the age of 56, he walked from Preston to London to attend a Temperance Convention. Ironically this was to be one of his final actions in support of the cause. He died a short time later on October 27th, 1846.

His funeral which took place on Sunday, 1st November, 1846 was a most impressive affair. A large number of 'Teetotallers' attended the funeral,

Richard 'Dicky' Turner – more drunk than sober – entered the Temperance Meeting. By the time he had left he had signed the pledge.

including groups from Wigan, Hindley, Bolton, Blackburn, Padiham and Lancaster. The 'Teetotallers' marched two-abreast and numbered in excess of four hundred as the streets through which the procession passed were thronged with spectators.

Laid to rest in St. Peter's graveyard, Preston, his gravestone was inscribed with the words: "Beneath this stone are deposited the remains of Richard Turner, Author of the word Teetotal. As applied to abstinence from all intoxicating liquors".

Exactly one hundred years later, Preston historian John H. Spencer, an admirer of the 19th-century movement, made a pilgrimage to 'Dicky' Turner's grave in the old burial ground of St. Peter's Church. On a bleak cold morning, as heavy clouds hung from the sky, he stood at the graveside a solitary pilgrim, and brushing autumn leaves from the flat grave slab he revealed once again the inscription chiselled a century before. The word 'Teetotal' had been a beacon for the movement and had spread like a flaming crusade throughout the kingdom and the United States.

Richard Turner – Born 20th July 1790 – Died 27th October 1846.

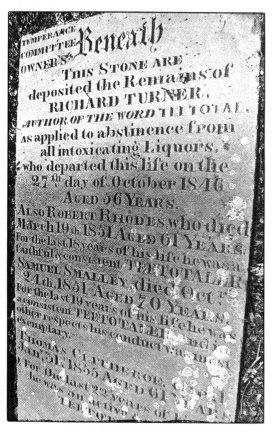

Richard Turner's gravestone in St. Peter's churchyard recalls his connection with the Temperance movement.

Postscript:
Not all the Temperance advocates were thought of as highly as Richard Turner. In September, 1848, three of their members appeared before the magistrates on a charge of assaulting Mrs. Hunter, the landlady of the Star and Garter public house in Brook Street.

In the course of some speeches which were delivered against intoxicating liquor, it would seem that certain allusions were made which were construed as personal by Mrs. Hunter. In consequence she rushed through the crowd and pulled the speaker off the chair on which he was standing. The Teetotallers, it seems, did not behave with all the forebearance which might have been expected and Mrs. Hunter, finding herself assaulted, sought redress by summoning Thomas Eccles, Thomas Walley and George Dearden before the magistrates.

The defendants called witnesses with a view to proving that Mrs. Hunter was drunk at the time. One witness stating that when the landlady rushed through the crowd gathering opposite her public house, she "smelt for all the world like a gin cask".

The presiding magistrate reminded the Temperance advocates that he could not allow the peace to be broken by them and that the occupants of the Star and Garter had rent and taxes to pay, and a living to earn. Their decision, he felt, to hold a meeting opposite to a public house, was calculated to create a breach of the peace.

In conclusion the defendants were each ordered to pay costs and cautioned to be more careful in the future.

Sources:
 'Preston Chronicle', November 1846
 'Preston Herald', December 1946

Chapter 8

PRIVATE WILLIAM YOUNG

See the Conquering Hero Comes

On December 22nd, 1915 Private William Henry Young of the East Lancashire Regiment was serving on the Western Front. Looking out from his trench he spotted his company sergeant lying wounded in 'no man's land'. Disregarding the enemy's fire he scrambled over the trench parapet to go to the aid of the non-commissioned officer. The wounded officer requested that Private Young get under cover, but he refused and was almost immediately wounded himself, having his jaw shattered by a German bullet.

Notwithstanding his terrible injuries, Private Young continued endeavouring to effect the rescue upon which he had set his mind, and eventually he succeeded with the aid of another soldier. His mission accomplished, he then walked unaided to the dressing station, where it was discovered that he had also been wounded by a rifle bullet in the chest. He was at once admitted to a military hospital and eventually brought back to England.

The wound to his chest did not prove serious, but the damaged jaw called for surgical attention and he was admitted to hospitals in Exeter, London and Aldershot, where he was operated on two or three times with apparently satisfactory results.

In his home town, news eventually filtered through of his heroics on the Western Front and when it was revealed that his actions were to be recommended as worthy of the Victoria Cross, a great deal of excitement was generated.

The official record stated that he had acted with great fortitude, determination, courage and devotion to duty, which could hardly have been surpassed. As soon as the award of the Victoria Cross was confirmed the local newspaper headlines blazed the good news.

At last, in the middle of April, 1916 although not fully recovered, he was considered well enough to spend a few days leave in his home town. A welcome 'befitting a king' greeted Private Young as he stepped from the train at Preston Railway Station.

Winter on the Western Front, 1915

The main streets of the town were bedecked with bunting for his homecoming and a military band played 'See the Conquering Hero Comes', as he was carried shoulder-high and placed in a carriage provided by the Mayor, Harry Cartmell. For the journey to the Town Hall, soldiers removed the horse from its carriage and themselves pulled the conveyance through the cheering crowds that lined the route.

The official welcome afforded to him in the Market Square was witnessed by an enthusiastic multitude. Amongst those who joined in the plaudits were seven of his nine young children, who were awaiting him on the balcony of the Town Hall.

When the official proceedings ended, the hero was driven through a cheering throng to his terraced home in Heysham Street. The street, and his house, were transformed with decorations by his proud neighbours.

Alderman Harry Cartmell, Mayor, had officially announced to the people of Preston the award of William Young's Victoria Cross by the launching of an appeal to support his wife and nine children which read as follows: "Town Hall Preston.

You will doubtless have heard of the wonderful deeds of bravery performed by Pte. William Young, of the East Lancashire Regiment, for which he has gained the Victoria Cross. This has brought distinction upon the town, and I am sure that it will be the general feeling that our appreciation should be expressed in some substantial way. The fact that Pte. Young has a family of nine children will, I think, emphasise the appeal I now make for a substantial money presentation. The exact form the gift will take will be considered later at a meeting of subscribers. I shall be glad to receive subscriptions."

Within a month over £500 had been raised, sufficient to provide his family with an income of 10 shillings per week from the interest on the money's investment. During the whole of his week-long stay he was greeted with acclaim. Local cinemas and theatres invited him as guest-of-honour. His leave complete, the likeable war hero had to return to hospital for further tests and observation.

By the middle of August he appeared to be progressing very well, and it was decided that one further minor operation on his jaw would be beneficial. After a few days home leave he returned to Aldershot for routine surgery. During this operation things went tragically wrong: the chloroform appeared to affect his heart. While he lay in an unconscious state, a telegram was sent to his wife who immediately dashed to his bedside. She arrived within hours and the following morning, Sunday, 27th August, 1916 he passed away in Cambridge Hospital, Aldershot.

Apparently he had been poorly after his other anaesthetics and every precaution was taken during the operation. As little chloroform as possible had been administered and that had been undertaken by a highly experienced doctor. In all, five doctors saw him and did what was possible.

One of his commanding officers in writing to express his sympathy remarked, "that it seemed so terribly cruel to go through all he did and so well, only to die through the worst of bad luck".

His bravery still fresh in the minds of Preston's inhabitants, was remembered once again as he was given a military funeral from his home in Heysham Street. His coffin, draped in the Union Jack, was borne on a gun carriage to English Martyrs' Church and then to Preston Cemetery.

The coffin of the First World War hero was draped in the Union Jack and borne on a gun carriage - vast crowds paid silent homage.

Again, large crowds lined the route but this time the cheers were replaced by silent homage. At the graveside, rifle volleys were fired as the 'Last Post' sounded. The war hero was laid to rest in the town where he had lived and loved unlike so many fallen heroes, destined to lay buried in a foreign land.

A few months later his widow attended Buckingham Palace to receive the Victoria Cross on behalf of her late husband. King George V presented the award and spoke of the Preston war hero's bravery and courage.

Postscript: Seventy years later in 1986, the eldest son of Private William Young, V.C., also named William, gave the much cherished Victoria Cross to the Queen's Lancashire Regiment. With their headquarters in the town, he thought it fitting that they should be entrusted with its safe keeping.

William Young, junior, a resident of Bexley Heath, Sussex, was with his mother when she received the award. He had enlisted in his father's old regiment when he was 14 years old and served as a private for a number of years. Throughout his military career, however, he felt somewhat overshadowed by his father's glory.

Sources:
  'Preston Guardian', September 1916
  For Remembrance by H. Cartmell, 1920

Preston's heroic soldier lies in Preston Cemetery – beneath a cross that records his bravery in the face of the enemy.

Chapter 9

ROBERT SERVICE
'Bard of the Yukon'

In the latter years of the last century prospecting and exploration became a way of life for many adventurers. The year 1898 being identified as the year of the Yukon Gold Rush. The activity that took place has long since past, yet the events that occurred still remain memorable - thanks in no small way to a Preston born poet.

That person being Robert Service, who was born in Christian Road, Preston on the 16th January, 1874. His father, a Scot, also named Robert was a bank clerk and his mother, Emily, was English. At the tender age of five, young Robert was whisked away to Scotland, never again to see the town of his birth. His only memory of the place was said to be the fact that he wore kilts and thus greatly attracted the attention of Prestonians more than otherwise would have been the case.

His mother is said to have inherited some ten thousand pounds from her father, an owner of cotton mills; an inheritance which prompted Mr. Service to give up his employment in a bank and move his family back to Glasgow.

After the move back to Scotland, the family grew to a total of seven boys and three girls. For a while to ease the crowded household, young Robert was sent to Ayrshire to live with grandfather Service and three maiden aunts, who were deeply religious people. It was with them that he is said to have made his first poetic utterance. The occasion was his sixth birthday and the supper table was spread like a feast. There was ham, cookies, scones and cakes and as they prepared to eat he asked Grandpa if he could say grace. Bowing his head reverently, he recited:

"God bless the cakes and bless the jam;
Bless the cheese and the cold boiled ham;
Bless the scones Aunt Jeannie makes,
And save us all from belly-aches. Amen".

After some years living with them he rejoined his parents in Glasgow. When he left school, aged 14, he entered a Scottish bank, where he was employed for seven years.

He became an avid reader and he indulged in light verse which he submitted to boys' magazines and to local papers. By the time he was sixteen he had contributed over twenty poems to weekly periodicals and never had a single one rejected.

It was a happy period of his life and with a book of poems in hand he would walk through the park, lingering in pleasant places, dreaming and reciting.

The peak of his poetic taste he found in Tennyson and Browning; he had to be in the proper mood for Wordsworth and Milton, while it took an effort for him to enjoy Keats and Shelley.

In his early twenties he uplifted his roots and embarked for Canada where he spent seven years on a backwoods ranch on the edge of the primeval forest. It was at a time when man's usefulness was measured in his ability to do hard physical work and Robert Service toiled to be an accepted member of that society.

Graduating from what he described as the "college of hard knocks" he then spent a short time in California, following that with a tramping tour of Mexico.

Once again Canada beckoned and, with a reference from his former Scottish banking employers, he gained employment with the Canadian Bank of Commerce. After a short period in the city bank he was sent to a place called Whitehorse, in the Yukon territory.

It was late in 1904 when he arrived there and the peak of the Yukon Gold Rush had been in 1898. Infact, prospecting and exploration had begun there before he was born.

Although winter began soon after he arrived he found himself entering one of the most satisfying periods of his life. The country captivated him and he came to both know it and love it deeply. The bank manager, who had been an adventurous sea captain, was a good talker and he soon taught Service the use of the Yukon vernacular.

For Service the bank clerk it was a busy time, yet outside office hours he had plenty of time for loafing and dreaming. He became a lover of the long and lonely walk and soon realised the poetry in his surrounds before he discovered the words.

Never was life so wonderful as when he went on those long trails in temperatures normally 40 degrees below freezing, accompanied by his little cocker spaniel and a big stick.

The urge to write began to dominate his thoughts and on one of those trails he began to piece together in his mind a ballad that was to change his life. The setting was a saloon with two guys preparing for a showdown. Hurrying back to his living quarters above the bank, he penned the 'Shooting of Dan McGrew'. The dramatic ballad was the beginning of a long series of verses contained in five books of poems, of which his first two 'Songs of a Sourdough' and 'Ballads of a Cheechako' were acclaimed the best.

One of his ambitions had been to build up a personal nest-egg in his savings account and the publication of his works soon assured his future prosperity. His books were at once immensely popular in Canada and America and later in the country of his birth.

From that first ballad the words flowed freely and rare was the day that he did not write something. Altogether he spent eight years in the Yukon and later described them as the years he most would have liked to live over again. His verse undoubtedly helped to make the Yukon era a memorable one.

Besides becoming famous as a poet, Service developed his ability as a novelist. His books were extremely well written and entertaining. The first one 'The Trail of '98', was published in 1910. It gives the history of the great gold rush in 1898 and is full of passion and jealousy. Bringing the wild west to life it features the reckless, hardy pioneers and the brutal, cunning thieves, vagabonds and desparadoes of the time. The saloon bar, the gambling den and the rowdy dance halls, all feature in the Yukon's story.

In all Robert Service's life was a full one and he never gave up his ties with the veteran sourdoughs (prospectors) of the Yukon trail.

Before the First World War he married a French girl called Germaine and when hostilities broke out he drove an ambulance for the Red Cross. Later he is believed to have been connected with the Canadian Army and its intelligence department.

Between the wars, he lived mainly in France, but was forced to flee the country during the Second World War. He returned there for his final years.

Service's autobiography, published in 1946, was entitled 'Ploughman of the Moon'. It dealt with the first forty years of his life and was acclaimed as one of the year's better autobiographical works.

His verses continued to be published regularly up until his death in September, 1958. In January of that year he wrote to his New York publisher and included the following amusing verse:

"Alas! My belly is concave,
My locks no longer wavy,
But though I've one foot in the grave   Robert Service,
The other's in the gravy.   crowding eightyfour".

Right to the end of his life he wrote in the blood and guts style that made him famous. His philosophy was that it is not what we make with our hands and brains that matter, but what we make with ourselves.

Robert Service – Born January 1874 – Died 1958.

Postscript:

In 1974, the centenary year of the birth of Preston born poet, Robert William Service, tentative enquiries were made with the occupiers of no. 4 Christian Road, Preston with a view to placing a plaque outside the house, to mark the poet's birthplace.

Unfortunately, the Council's approach came to nothing as residents of the terraced row firstly requested the Council to repair pavements, damaged by container lorries using the thoroughfare and secondly, by them requesting the

Robert Service – his blood and guts style of writing led to fame.

removal of yellow parking lines that prevented them from parking their vehicles outside their homes.

Ironically, a little while later it was discovered that the house the Klondyke bard was born in was infact on the other side of the road. The confusion had arisen due to a renumbering of the houses in Christian Road around about 1887. At that time the house that was no. 4 was changed to no. 9.

Due to the fact that the newly discovered birthplace of the poet was on the side of the road earmarked for demolition, nothing further was done about the placing of a plaque. Now the house has been demolished and an office complex stands on the site.

Sources:
  'Songs in Autumn'
  'Preston Herald', 1947
  'Ploughman of the Moon', 1946

In his poetry Robert Service called upon his experiences of life — one such example being the following verse from his poem —

THE JOY OF BEING POOR

Let others sing of gold and gear, the joy of being rich;
But oh, the days when I was poor, a vagrant in a ditch!
When every dawn was like a gem, so radiant and rare,
And I had but a single coat, and not a single care;
When I would feast right royally on bacon, bread and beer,
And dig into a stack of hay and doze like any peer;
When I would wash beside a brook my solitary shirt,
And though it dried upon my back I never took a hurt;
When I went romping down the road contemptuous of care,
And slapped Adventure on the back — by Gad! we were a pair;
When, though my pockets lacked a coin, and though my coat was old,
The largess of the stars was mine, and all the sunset gold;
When time was only made for fools, and free as air was I,
And hard I hit and hard I lived beneath the open sky;
When all the roads were one to me, and each had its allure . . .
Ye Gods! these were the happy days, the days when I was poor.

Chapter 10

FRANCIS THOMPSON

Made All Men His Debtors

In August, 1910 a stone tablet bearing the inscription 'Francis Joseph Thompson was born in this house, December, 1859' was placed in position on the outside of no. 7 Winckley Street, Preston. It was the gift of Mrs. Catherine Holiday, formerly of Preston, and was the outcome of her desire to see the birthplace of the great Preston born poet perpetuated. The tablet, neat and simple in appearance, with its clear Roman type of lettering, was the work of a stonemason from Ulverston.

Francis Thompson was the son of Doctor Charles Thompson and his wife Mary Turner Thompson (formerly Morton). All the children of the marriage were born in Preston; two babies, a boy and a girl, being buried in the town.

While the surviving children were young, Dr. Thompson moved to Ashton-under-Lyne. In September, 1870 at the start of a new school year Francis Thompson was sent to the Catholic College of Ushaw in County Durham. His chief successes during his college studies were in English and essay writing. While at Ushaw he developed a talent for verse and was a lover of the written word. His companions of the time recalled his love of books and watching cricket; although he showed no interest in participating in sporting activities himself.

Altogether he spent seven years at Ushaw and its religious atmosphere influenced his life deeply. He was next sent to Owens College, Manchester to study medicine. Alas, the subject had little attraction for him, and he preferred to frequent the public libraries of Manchester rather than dedicate his time to medical studies. In the end, unwilling to pursue his studies to his father's liking, he left home and settled in London, without prospects, friends or means.

The story of this period of his life is sad reading. He became the wreck of poverty and took to opium. For a while he was an assistant in a shop, later a collector for a bookseller.

At last one of his poems was accepted for publication and through it the poet was discovered by friends willing and anxious to assist. The poem was received by the editor of 'Merrie England', a former fellow student at Ushaw, who recognised the merit of the work. After a long search he found the author whose days in the slums and haunts of poverty were thenceforth over.

After being carefully nursed, Francis Thompson lived for a while at Storrington, in Sussex. He was befriended by Mr. Wilfred Meynell, and he and his family became the subject of some of the poet's finest verses. He was greatly encouraged by Mrs. Meynell, who herself was a poet and one of the most distinguished female writers of the period.

The first volume of Thompson's poems which appeared in 1893, under the simple title 'Poems', attracted attention immediately. One of the longer pieces 'The Hounds of Heaven' the critics did not hesitate to say, was the most wonderful lyric in the English language. He was at once acclaimed as the equal of Shelley, a worthy disciple of Dantes and a Crashaw cast in a diviner mould.

Then in 1895 a volume entitled 'Sister Songs', written in praise of two little sisters appeared on the scene. "A book which Shelley would have adored", wrote one authority about the volume that contained a number of lovely and most musical lines. When his next volume of poems appeared under the title 'New Poems', the critics once again sang his praises, saying that his high mark of genius was once again evident.

Thompson was also a popular writer and his prose was said to be as sonorous and full of charm as his poems. He contributed many valuable reviews on history, biography and travel to the leading magazines of the day.

The later years of his life were comparatively uneventful, save for his writings, which brought him into contact with many of the great literateurs of the day.

For some years before his death he was a familiar figure in the streets of London. He would wander about, apparently in aimless fashion, but in reality absorbed in his own thoughts. Often enough he could be seen clad (winter and summer alike) in a brown cloak with a basket slung around his shoulders, in which he carried the books he had to review.

His death occurred in November, 1907 from consumption the ravages of which he had long suffered. For the last few years of his life he had but one lung and was terribly emaciated. At the time of entering the London hospital, where he died, he weighed just five stone. The devoted nurse who attended him stated that he was a very quiet and unselfish person. The sorrow of his early days had endeared him to his friends and his passing was deeply mourned.

In prefacing the volume of 'Thompson's Selected Poems', his good friend Mr. Meynell wrote: "He made all men his debtors, leaving to those who loved him the memory of a unique personality and to English poetry, an imperishable name".

> "I hang 'mid men my needless head,
> And my fruit is dreams, as theirs is bread,
> The goodly men and the sun hazed sleeper,
> Time shall reap; but after the reaper,
> The world shall glean of me, me the sleeper!"

So wrote Francis Thompson who, so long as the English Language lasts, will ensure Preston's place on the literary map.

Postcript:

In later years the stone tablet outside his birthplace was replaced by a commemorative bronze plaque which includes a likeness of the much admired poet. Exactly one hundred years after his birth the President of Preston Poet Society hung a laurel wreath on the wall of no. 7 Winckley Street and spoke of "The town's honour to its prophet."

Francis Thompson – Born December 1859 – Died November 1907.

Sources:
  'Preston Guardian'
  20 August 1910
  F. Thompson Biography
  c.1922
  'Preston Guardian'
  November 1913
  'Preston Herald' 1944

The birthplace of Preston poet Francis Thompson, No. 7 Winckley Street, is marked with a plaque.

A critic of the early 20th century had this to say of Francis Thompson's work – 'In sheer power of expression Thompson is occasionally unsurpassable. We have not to travel far to meet with gorgeous imagery and astonishing splendours of diction. Though he is great in snatches there are poems of his in which there is sustained and cumulative power. Nothing like the 'Hound of Heaven' has been written in modern times. It makes a great appeal both through the glories of its style and the lesson that underlies it.' The 'Hound of Heaven' includes the following verses:

> Now of that long pursuit
> Come on at hand the bruit;
> That Voice is round me like a bursting sea;
> "And is thy earth so marred
> Shattered in shard on shard?
> Lo, all things fly thee, for thy fliest Me!
> Strange, piteous, futile thing!
> Wherefore should any set thee love apart?
> Seeing none but I make much of naught" (He said),
> "And human love needs human meriting!"
> How hast thou merited —
>
> Of all man's clotted clay, the dingiest clot?
> Alack, thou knowest not
> How little worthy of any love thou art!
> Whom wilt thou and to love ignoble thee,
> Save Me, save only Me?
> All which I took from thee I did but take
> Not for thy charms,
> But just that thou might seek it in My arms.
> All which thy child's mistake
> Fancies as lost, I have stored for thee at home;
> Rise, clasp My hand, and come!

The Bishop of London described 'The Hound of Heaven' as one of the most tremendous poems ever written. Its subject being God's pursuit – as the Hound – of the fleeing and resisting soul, and eventually the recovery of the latter.

The critic from the 'Bookman' publication described Francis Thompson thus –
"In all sobriety do we believe him of all poets to be the most celestial in vision, the most august in faculty . . . these are big words, but we have weighed them."

The poem 'Contemplation' which includes the following verse highlights his acute awareness of his surroundings, earthly or otherwise.

This morning saw I, fled the shower,
The earth reclining in a lull of power:
The heavens, pursuing not their path,
Lay stretched out naked after bath,
Or so it seemed; field, water, tree, were still,
Nor was there any purpose on the calm-browed hill.
The hill, which sometimes visibly is
Wrought with unresting energies,
Looked idly; from the musing wood,
And every rock, a life renewed
Exhaled like an unconscious thought
When poets, dreaming unperplexed,
Dream that they dream of naught.
Nature one hour appears a thing unsexed,
Or to such serene balance brought
That her twin natures cease their sweet alarms,
And sleep in one another's arms.
The sun with resting pulses seems to brood,
And slacken its command upon my unurged blood.

Chapter 11

REV. ROBERT &
EDMUND HARRIS

The Vicar and the Benefactor

On Wednesday 30th May, 1877 the 'Preston Guardian' newspaper announced to its readers the death of local solicitor and former Prothonotary for Lancashire, Edmund Robert Harris. In his 73rd year, he had died the previous Sunday morning at his residence, Whinfield House, Ashton-on-Ribble.

For several years he had been in failing health and as the infirmities of age manifested themselves he was forced to relinquish the more active duties of his life. During the early Spring of his final year his health had seemed to take a turn for the better. However, the bitter east winds that prevailed towards the end of May led to him catching a chill. Exposed to the cold he suffered a worsening in his bronchial condition and on the last Sunday in May, he passed away.

No sooner was the death of the last member of the Harris family announced than speculation began to emerge concerning his family's fortune. Calculated as being upwards of £250,000 it was the subject of much public curiosity. The fact that Edmund Harris had no lineal descendants led to a popular appetite for information.

Rumours abounded and speculators had soon divided the vast legacy. Local Charities were to receive a mere pittance with the bulk of the estate being left to 'Queen Anne's Bounty', a trust for the augmentation of the livings of the poor clergymen.

The funeral of Edmund Harris was intended in all respects to be a private one, the mourners being only those intimately associated with him during his lifetime. Despite a morning of drenching showers the church of St. Andrew's, Ashton was packed with those eager to pay their last respects. In fitting manner the deceased was laid to rest in the family vault alongside his younger brother Thomas, who had died two years previously. The bachelor brothers had been associated with the Ashton church from the time they had moved to their Whinfield residence to enjoy their retirement years.

The Harris family connections with the town of Preston had begun in 1788, when the Rev. Robert Harris, B.D. was appointed headmaster of Preston Grammar School, which in those days was situated in Stoneygate. On average, the school had forty scholars and the new headmaster received an annual salary of about £100.

Edmund Robert Harris - his death in May 1877 led to speculation concerning his family's fortune

The son of a goods carrier, he was born in Clitheroe in 1764 and was educated firstly at Clitheroe Grammar School and secondly at Sidney College, Cambridge. An eager young man, he soon became a member of the inner circle of the gentry, as his membership of Preston's Oyster and Parched Pea Club confirmed. Originally it was a very select affair, with the chief business of the assembled members being wine drinking and oyster eating.

In 1797 he was appointed as Vicar of St. George's Church, combining his new duties with his role as headmaster of the town's leading education establishment.

Around the turn of the century romance blossomed in his busy life and he married a local girl called Ann Lodge. She was the sister of two of Preston's most prominent solicitors, Edmund and Jonathan Lodge.

The marriage was a fruitful one and within a few years his wife had borne him four children. Sadly, the first child died in infancy. Happily soon followed Edmund Robert, born in 1803, Thomas born in 1804, and a daughter Ellen Elizabeth born in 1806.

The congregation of St. George's church had a great affection for the Rev. Harris and he was known by the humbler classes as 'Parson' Harris, a term of endearment that they bestowed upon him.

Conscious of the need to secure the future of his sons he arranged for them to serve their apprenticeships with their uncles's firm of solicitors, which was originally in the Old Cock Yard. The placement of the sons was a success and both became partners once they had proved themselves. The firm then became known as Lodge and Harris and took over premises at 14 Chapel Street.

Originally the Harris household resided at what we now know as Arkwright House, in Stoneygate. This building having been erected for the specific purpose of housing the headmaster of the Grammar School. When he relinquished control of the school in 1835, he was obliged to vacate those premises and the family moved to 16 Ribblesdale Place.

Within a couple of years his wife died, aged 64 and, along with his two sons and daughter, he moved the short distance to 13

St George's Church, Preston, for sixty-four years 'Parson' Harris preached from its pulpit.

Ribblesdale Place. In this time of sorrow the Vicar was comforted by his spinster daughter as he continued to devote his time to the well-being of his flock at St. George's church.

The family was settled in the Winckley Square area of the town and Ellen Elizabeth and her brothers were often seen out horse-riding which was her great passion. The first requirement of any would-be suitor for the Vicar's daughter was said to be equinary skill.

All continued well for the family until 1849, when the Rev. Harris suffered a further blow with the death of his devoted daughter in her 43rd year. The Vicar felt the loss of her and his health declined for some time afterwards.

As incumbent of St. George's he continued to administer to his congregation and among the gifts bestowed on him were silverware and oil paintings of himself. He was at ease in the pulpit of his church and his sermons were preached with vigour and energy. One of his most outstanding sermons was made on Christmas Day, 1861. The 'cotton famine' was at that time beginning to be felt and fierce and bitter strife was on the horizon. Displaying all the fire and impressiveness of an old veteran he delivered his message of righteousness, directed at rich and poor alike.

As things transpired, that Christmas morning message was to be the final one from the man said to be the town's oldest inhabitant, twelve days later he died. The aged patriarch was in his 98th year. Death brought to an end an unparalleled period of sixty-four years as Vicar of St. George's.

It was necessary to obtain special permission from the Home Secretary for him to be buried in the graveyard of his beloved St. George's. His wish was granted and he was laid to rest alongside his wife and the two children who had pre-deceased him.

The surviving sons, Edmund Robert and Thomas Harris were obviously not short of money, as their building of Whinfield House indicated. The source of their wealth has always been of interest and John H. Spencer, a respected historian in the middle of this century, often answered the query in the following manner:

"The brothers were lawyers as were their uncles, that there was never a poor lawyer except in fiction, and that no doubt the brothers' got the bulk of their uncles' money".

When Thomas Harris died, his money was inherited by his elder brother, who ended up with possession of the family's entire wealth. It is believed that the bulk of the Harris fortune was made by shrewd and timely investments in railway shares.

Edmund Robert Harris was a man whose aim was to do what he had to do well, humbly, quietly and without ostentation. He preferred to walk the secluded paths of life rather than tread the thoroughfares that lead to fame and glory. He had already shown his benevolent nature by providing the money for the Harris Infectious Ward, a crucial part of the town's Infirmary.

His Will made twelve months before his death had certainly kept the rumour mongers busy. The eagerly awaited reading of the document showed that he had certainly not neglected the town of his birth. It was a Will that would ensure the name of Harris had a permanent place in Preston's history.

Practically the whole of the fortune was devoted to religious, educational and philanthropic causes. His intention was to bestow all he had, so that work his father had tried to do could be continued. He gave the trustees wide discretionary powers in the administration of his great estate and they co-operated fully, to carry out the spirit as well as the letter of Edmund Robert Harris's pious intention.

The Corporation gladly accepted a gift of £122,000 for the erection of The Harris Free Library, Art Gallery & Museum. They provided the site adjacent to the Market Place at a cost of £30,000 and furnished it with the books of the existing Free Library and of Dr. Shepherd's reference library. The art collection and museum from the old Literary and Philosophical Institute was also centralised and the Corporation agreed to undertake the upkeep and maintenance of the building and its contents.

The Harris Trustees were also instructed to use £100,000 for the establishment of the Harris Orphanage. This home opened in 1888, on a site purchased in Fulwood, and for almost a hundred years provided a disciplined, yet caring home for orphaned children.

The third main beneficiary was the Harris Institute and Technical College which received over £78,000. This educational establishment had begun as the Institution for the Diffusion of Knowledge and later became the Avenham Institute. With the aid of the Harris money it became the Harris Technical College in Corporation Street, which is now, of course, the University of Central Lancashire.

Today its buildings are spread all over town and they include the Harris Orphanage buildings which closed in 1983. A great believer in educational opportunities, Edmund Robert Harris would be both astonished and delighted at the progress made by the Harris Technical College.

The churches were not forgotten. A legacy of over £7,000 going to the improvement of The Protestant Churches in the town. For the Preston Grammar School, there was a sum of £3,000, for the foundation of scholarships, and for the Institution for the Blind there was a payment of £500.

In all, with bequests to servants, clerks and friends, the fortune amounted to over £300,000. A man with simple tastes, regarded by his servants as a kind and considerate master, he turned out to be one of Preston's greatest benefactors.

Postscript:
No. 13 Ribblesdale Place where the Harris family resided for a number of years, was later occupied by Joseph Toulmin, cheese factor and brother of George Toulmin of the 'Preston Guardian'. Under the terms of the Will of one of the later occupants, the premises became The Vicarage for the Rector of Preston.

Sources:
'PrestonGuardian' June 1877
'Preston Guardian' January 1862
'Preston Herald' May 1944
Hewitson's History of Preston

The Harris brothers are laid to rest in St. Andrew's graveyard in Ashton.

Chapter 12

Edith Rigby, Secretary of the
Preston Suffragette movement

EDITH RIGBY

'The woman as much
as the man'

In the years preceding the First World War the slogan 'VOTES FOR WOMEN' was always at the forefront of local and national politics. Preston, during this period, had its share of excitement relative to the campaign, with the local branch of the organisation very active.

All the organisation of the Preston branch and its early meetings was done from no. 28 Winckley Square. There lived Edith Rigby, the wife of Doctor Charles Rigby and when the branch was formed about 1907, she was appointed as secretary.

Mrs. Rigby was Preston born, her birthplace was no. 1 Pole Street, and she was the sister of Doctor Arthur Rayner, a well known surgeon, physician and radiologist at the old Preston Royal Infirmary.

As the suffrage campaign gained momentum, Edith Rigby was in her early thirties and was an educated and intelligent woman. An acquaintance of hers was Preston historian, John H. Spencer who was co-secretary with her of the Arkwright Debating Society. In an article in the 'Preston Herald' he described her in the following manner -

"She dressed plainly and simply and had a frank open face. Her dark brown hair was brushed tightly away from her forehead and rolled neatly in a little coil at the back of her head. She had firm, delicate features and when she opened her mouth in humourous smile, she displayed natural teeth perfect in their setting. Her eyes were clear and soft, full of sympathy and lit up her face when talking. Her whole appearance suggested a lady of unassuming and quiet demeanour and her general behaviour and manners added to her appeal. She had indomitable will power and once she was convinced of the righteousness of votes for women, nothing would turn her from her purpose.

Opposition only fired her zeal and made her more enthusiastic then ever. She was a brave woman and scorned danger to satisfy her conscience".

The inspirer of the movement for the enfranchisement and social liberty of women was Mrs. Pankhurst, and she was beloved by all her followers, none being more loyal than the Preston Secretary. She joined in many of the protest meetings and marches organised by the suffragettes and, like so many of her colleagues, she suffered a number of terms of imprisonment for her more militant activities.

Locally there were many headline making activities that Mrs. Rigby and her colleagues organised. A political meeting at the Public Hall ended in pandemonium as two suffragettes, one of them Mrs. Rigby, chained themselves to seats and proudly proclaimed the battle cry, 'Votes for Women'. Their reward was to be unceremoniously handled by the police and mocked and sneered at by the gathering.

Acid was poured on the greens of Fulwood Golf course and a fire was lighted on the stands of Blackburn Rovers Football Club, stones were thrown at political gatherings, politicians were threatened with horse-whips and broken glass was often followed by the suffragettes battle cry.

What the women sought was the greatest social change which Great Britain had ever known. It was not simply a claim for the vote, but a claim for equality –

"I sing the man and the woman
And the woman as much as the man".

No longer did they wish to be ruled by the old proverb, "The woman's kingdom is her home". After all, such a kingdom was subject externally to political influences.

Until the summer of 1913 the Movement's progress was steady, if not spectacular. However, in May of that year a bill which proposed to confer the Parliamentary franchise upon women who were householders, or wives of householders, and over 25 years of age, was rejected by a majority of some 50 votes. There were those who said the result had been contributed to by the excesses of the suffragettes and the exploits of a little band of ill-balanced and fanatical women. Within days the suffrage movement rolled into action and locally the summer was to be dominated by the activities of Edith Rigby and her campaigning colleagues.

The first local action that hit the headlines appeared in the 'Preston Guardian' of Saturday, May 17th. Under the heading "Act of Vandalism in a Preston park", appeared a report of the disfiguring of the Derby statue in Miller Park. The monument to the 19th century politician had been defaced by the spraying of a liquid substance resembling tar, which disfigured the chest, body and legs. The action had taken place the previous weekend during the hours that the park was closed to the public.

Tied to a rose tree near the statue was a luggage label and on it was pasted a newspaper cutting referring to agitation for women's suffrage. A reward of £50 was immediately offered for information leading to the conviction of those responsible.

The local suffragettes were suspected of being responsible for the outrage, although the culprits were never discovered.

As the treatment meted out to the suffragettes became harsher so their resolve hardened and more militant action followed. The doctor's wife was even more determined in her resolve and in July, 1913 she was held responsible for two actions that shocked the residents of Preston and the County of Lancashire.

In the first week of the month she was instrumental in causing a terrific explosion at the Exchange Buildings, Liverpool. Although no one was injured by the explosion a considerable amount of damage was caused.

Then a couple of days later she was responsible for the burning down of the then Sir William Lever's desirable Roynton Cottage on the Rivington Estate. Armed with paraffin she started a number of fires around the property and, in the dry summer conditions, the timber bungalow was soon ablaze.

Within days, with the police enquiries underway, Edith Rigby calmly walked into the Liverpool police station and surrendered herself.

She made a long statement and was taken before the Magistrates the following morning. During the proceedings which were concerned primarily with the explosion at the cotton exchange, she made a lengthy reply which included the following:

> "I did this on my own planning. I only told one minor official of the Union what I was proposing to do. I placed the explosives in the Liverpool Exchange, and I want you to realise when women are driven to these desperate measures that they would so much rather adopt other measures; also how comparatively easy it is for women to get explosives and place them in public places. Of course, if I wished I could just as easily have placed that bomb under your Nelson statue where it would be bound to hurt people all round, but I wanted to

place it where there was the least possible risk for myself or anybody else. There was some risk I know, and I took it. The whole week previously and days before I had had it in my mind, walking about wishing it most devoutly. Perhaps you don't realise how much I thought that this should not hurt anyone unless it was myself. As the thing happened I went down into the deeper basement of the passage, of which I knew nothing. I thought I was putting it down a grating. It was part of my wishes and intense desire not to hurt anybody. By your kind and efficient officer I was asked what reasons I had to hurt the merchants of the Cotton Exchange, and I say this reason – that this great cotton industry is built up very much on women's labour. These merchants who are willing to get power and wealth on their labour, deny these women the vote; that they are being taxed all the time either directly or indirectly is nothing to the merchants of the Exchange. This was a knock at the door: the first knock they have had. Instead of giving myself up I could have yesterday written anonymously to the head of the Exchange, the head officer, or to your Lord Mayor but I preferred to come here to give myself up.

" I have another statement about another so-called fire to make. I want it to be told to the King and Sir Wm. Lever. I understand that Sir Wm. Lever is a vigorous man in all that he does, but he is an opponent to women's rights. I want to ask him whether he thinks his property on Rivington Pike was more valuable as one of his superfluous houses to be shown to important people and used occasionally, or as a beacon lighted for King and country to see, to show that there are some insupportable grievances of women? Though all women do not know that and feel that, we know that and feel that for the others, and we are acting for them.

"I do not know whether Sir William Lever has the same sense of spiritual value as he has of material, but if he has he will realise that valuable as all that piled up in the house was, that still more it is that women should have the right to help to remove the human sickness from England: to help to remove the different standards of moral uncleanness between men and women.

"As an opponent of women's suffrage, I wish to ask him as a challenge whether he thinks it is more useful as it stood or more useful now, a beacon light to those injustices which women feel they can support no longer. I lighted that fire alone that night and I did it alone."

Remanded in custody, she was content at having voiced her protests at the exploitation of women's labour in the cotton industry and the injustices of the political system. She was no stranger to the penal system and was forcibly fed on a number of occasions, having been an ardent hunger striker when either Walton Gaol or Strangeways played host to her. In fact, during the time of her July escapades she was on special leave from prison, the Government having abandoned forcible feeding and sent the suffragettes home to recover before completing their sentences.

Walton Gaol was again to be the scene of a hunger strike by her. This resulted in her returning to Winckley Square to be nursed back to health. Once she recovered she fled to Ireland for a brief spell. When she returned to Preston she led a protest at the Public Hall, and was re-arrested in unceremonious fashion.

As things transpired the suffragette campaigning was to take a back seat in 1914 with Europe on the brink of war. Mrs. Rigby, like all the other suffragettes, forgot her grievances and rallied round in support of the national cause. She became a member of the new Land Army and worked hard on a farm in Penwortham.

Finally, in 1918 those pioneering women were rewarded for their loyalty by the introduction of the 'Women's Franchise Bill'. Then a decade later the victory was complete, when the women of the country received full enfranchisement by the bill known at the time as 'The Flappers' Vote'.

Edith Rigby was a valiant woman who endured calumny and derision so that women of the present day might have votes and social equality with men. Her story can be read in a book entited 'My Aunt Edith', written by her niece, the poet, Phoebe Hesketh.

Historian John Spencer talked about a chance meeting with her half way up Penwortham Hill, one spring-time Sunday, during the war years. He recalled that there was no mention of the war or of the recent militant women's struggle. The talk was of books and writers, the sword of the suffragette propaganda had been sheathed and turned over to the farmer's ploughshare.

In all, Edith Rigby lived a long and useful life and she enjoyed her existence to the full, despite being an invalid in her latter years. She died in 1949 having served the cause of women's rights and been Preston's suffragette pioneer.

Postscript:
In fact, as long ago as November, 1867 Lily Maxwell, the proprietor of a shop that sold kitchenware, became the first woman to vote in a British Parliamentary election. In that year's Reform Act, which extended voting rights to less prosperous property owners, Mrs. Maxwell had her name erroneously added to the electoral roll.

On her way to cast her vote in the Manchester by-election she was escorted by a bodyguard of Liberal supporters and she duly voted in favour of their candidate, Jacob Bright, the victorious politician.

Mrs. Maxwell's success led to several more of Manchester's women property owners being successful in getting their names on the electoral register. The cry was for all property owning women to claim their vote.

In an attempt to stem the tide a court hearing was held and a year after Mrs. Maxwell's historic vote, the women's suffrage was declared illegal. That decision in November, 1868 meant a 50 year wait until the efforts of the suffragettes paid dividends.

Sources:
'Preston Guardian' May–July 1913
'Preston Herald' February 1943
'Preston Guardian' April 1906

Chapter 13

ROBERT CHARLES BROWN

Sixty-four Years a Doctor

Early in 1926 a great crowd assembled in Fishergate at the salerooms of Messrs. E.J. Reed and Sons. The reason was the auction of the residence of the late Sir Robert Charles Brown, a notable Preston physician. The premises 27, Winckley Square together with five motor garages at the rear, received an opening offer of £2,000. Bidding was brisk and the property was eventually sold for £4,550 the final bid being made by Councillor Oswald Aloysius Goodier, who was representing the authorities of the Preston Catholic College. The bidders included representatives of Preston Liberals whose last offer was £4,525.

According to the auctioneer the event was a significant one in Preston's history, the property being extremely well known as the birthplace and home of

Doctor Charles Brown – Brown Ward in the old Preston Royal Infirmary was named after this leading Preston surgeon.

Preston's 'Grand Old Man' for the majority of his life. The only time he lived away from the residence was for a ten year period beginning in 1855, when he was in London deeply engrossed in his medical studies.

The proceeds of the sale of the house and furniture were bequeathed by Dr. Brown to the Harris Orphanage. His Will was littered with charitable bequests and small legacies to personal friends and servants. Both his parlourmaid and cook received £100 legacies and further payments for each year of service.

Dr. Brown, who never married, died in November 1925 and the residue of the estate, which amounted to some £80,000 gross was divided into three equal parts. Two of them to be paid to the Board of Management of the Preston Royal Infirmary, for use in connection with the Convalescent Hospital at Lostock Hall. The remaining third to be invested by the trustees and the income paid to his sister, Mrs. Frances Margaret Hobbs during her life. Eventually after her death the money to be paid to the Preston Police Convalescent Home for Poor Children at Lytham.

Born in 1836, Charles Brown was a son of Dr. Robert Brown, and he had two brothers and four sisters. His eldest brother was the Rev. James Taylor Brown who was the vicar of Holy Trinity Church from 1867 until his death in 1875, at the age of 45. He left behind a widow and seven children, the eldest of whom was only 12 years of age. An eighth child was born a few months after his brother's death and consequently Charles Brown felt a great responsibility on his shoulders. The sudden death of a brother-in-law in 1889 left his sister a widow with eight children and further responsibility was imposed upon him.

In his Will Dr. Brown referred to his 17 nephews and nieces and to the fact that he had made gifts of money to each of them, at a time when it was most beneficial. He had, according to the Will, had the pleasure of receiving their personal thanks and had given each of them to understand there would be no further legacies after his death.

In his later years Dr. Brown wrote a book entitled 'Sixty Four Years A Doctor', and in it he related many personal recollections as an old Prestonian. He recalled the time spent as house surgeon to the old Preston Dispensary, and from 1870, as a member of staff at the Preston Royal Infirmary.

The crude methods of medical treatment employed in his early years, with patients being doped with opium or intoxicated with alcohol prior to surgery, are a reminder of the advances made from the days when a patient uttering piercing screams had to be held down by strong assistants.

One of Dr. Brown's roles was as the local medical officer to the London and North Western, and Lancashire and Yorkshire Railway Companies. He recalls the days prior to the opening of the Preston Royal Infirmary when any seriously injured railway workers had to be carried to one of the eleven beerhouses that were to be found in Butler Street, close to the railway station. There, the patient would remain until he either died or recovered sufficently to be removed to his home. Operations, such as the amputation of a limb, had to be performed in the most unsuitable places and on occasions only candle light shone on the harrowing scene. Once the Infirmary was opened however, many of the defects in the care and treatment of persons injured on the railways were remedied. However, there was no suitable conveyance for the removal to the Infirmary of those who were too seriously injured to ride in a cab. Consequently people walking the main streets of the town had to encounter

Dr R C Brown

MY OWN LIFE

I WAS born at 27, Winckley Square, Preston, on October 2, 1836, and, with the exception of an absence of ten years—1855 to 1865—I have lived in it for 75 years.

I was educated at the Preston Grammar School, under the Rev. George Nun Smith and the Rev. Edwin Smith, from 1845 to 1853. From 1853 to 1855 I was a medical pupil of Mr. Thomas Dixon, who lived at the Fishergate corner of Fox Street, and I went with him daily to the Preston Prison, of which he was the Visiting Surgeon. I also went every morning to the old Preston Dispensary to attend the practice in the out-patient department. In July, 1853, I passed a preliminary examination in Classics and Mathematics at the Apothecaries' Hall, Blackfriars Road, London, and in July, 1855, I was successful in passing the Matriculation Examination at the University of London. In October, 1855, I commenced my medical curriculum at King's College, London, and remained there until November, 1858, when I passed the examination at the Royal College of Surgeons of England and the Society of Apothecaries, and received my licences to practice.

The start of Doctor Robert Charles Brown's autobiography written in 1922, aged 86.

the unpleasant spectacle of some suffering creature, being carried shoulder high on a door or shutter by four or six men. Eventually Doctor Brown's efforts in collecting sufficent money enabled the purchase of a horse ambulance carriage to transport injured railway workers to the hospital.

Describing his early years at Winckley Square, Doctor Brown gave an insight into the running of a Victorian household. Along with his parents, two brothers and four sisters he was cared for by a domestic staff which consisted of a governess, nurse, cook, parlourmaid and housemaid. Their duties were typical of the servants of the period. The cook prepared four meals a day, the parlourmaid waited upon everyone except the two youngest children, the housemaid was responsible for making all the beds and all except the governess assisted in the weekly wash which commenced at one o'clock in the morning every Monday. They were woken by the nightwatchman, who patrolled the area and knocked them up by announcing the hour and the state of the weather.

There was not the luxury of the modern central heating systems and coals had to be carried up to the bedrooms from the cellars. Neither was there a regular visit from the window cleaner and with bucket and wash-leather the servants were expected to clean both the inside and outside of the windows. The lowest paid of the domestic staff was the nurse who received £8 a year for her labours.

Professionally Doctor Brown was regarded as one of Preston's leading surgeons and he was greatly concerned about the poor health of the town. This, he felt, was in no small part due to the inadequate domestic training given to young girls, who were put into the mills at an early age. As a result he believed they made very inadequate wives and mothers. He constantly urged the authorities in Preston to make domestic science a compulsory subject in elementary schools, and he finally succeeded before the turn of the century.

Always conscious of the need to ensure that the Infirmary was thoroughly up to date in equipment and resources, he often funded the purchases from his own finances. A new operating theatre at a cost of £2,700 was an example of his generosity.

In Doctor Brown's early days, there had been no trained nurses and consequently he treasured the skilled nursing staff around him at the Infirmary. Each year, as a reward for the nurses, he gave them a free day out in Fleetwood and Blackpool.

Important visitors were often entertained at his Winckley Square residence and he was always pleased to show them the places he was most proud of – Preston Royal Infirmary, Harris Museum and Art Gallery and the Harris Orphanage. A man with an abiding love of his native town he was always up and about before six o'clock in the morning, be it a Sunday or a weekday.

His outstanding medical career and his thoughtful generosity were recognised nationally and locally by the authorities of the time. The Town Council of Preston conferred their highest accolade on him by making him an Honorary Freeman of the Borough in 1910. While nationally he was eventually rewarded with a knighthood, a tribute to a compassionate Prestonian and his work and thought for others.

Sir Charles bequeathed his body to the directors of the Research Hospital of the Cambridge University, and authorised them to retain "such parts of it they may consider suitable additions to their pathological museum". He also requested them to place in their museum a glass bottle containing the ashes left by the cremation of his remains, "together with a statement of the weight of the ashes and my normal average weight, which has been eleven stones".

In recognition of his life a full civic memorial service was held in Preston Parish Church to record the passing of Preston's 'Grand Old Man'.

Robert Charles Brown – Born October, 1836 – Died November, 1925.

Sources:
  Will of Sir R. C. Brown 1927
  'Preston Guardian' 1910
  ' Preston Guardian' November 1915
  '64 Years a Doctor' R C Brown

Chapter 14

THOMAS LEYLAND

"No Soldier in the World to Lick the EnglishTommy"

Sometime in May, 1906 a reporter from the Preston Guardian newspaper with a pencil and notebook in hand, knocked on the door of a terraced house in Birchall Street, off Ribbleton Lane. When the door opened, he was greeted by a man in his seventies called Thomas Leyland. That day Mr. Leyland was away from his employment with local cotton spinners, Messrs. J & R. Smith, due to the fact that he was suffering from a heavy cold.

The reporter's mission was to hear first hand the events of half a century before, when the man who welcomed him into his house was fighting for Queen and country in the Crimean War. Mr. Leyland sat at one side of the kitchen fire in his rocking chair and his wife sat opposite, rocking one of their grandchildren in a cradle. Without wasting any time, Thomas Leyland began to recall his experiences in the army of the previous century.

The old soldier, who was born in Preston, told the reporter that after beginning his working life at the mill of John Goodairs, he had craved for adventure and decided to enlist. A tall, strapping fellow of sixteen years, he signed up with the 55th Regiment of Foot, which later became the Border Regiment. He was immediately sent to join the depot at Tralee, in County Kerry and it was there he spent the summer of 1853.

When the Crimea War broke out he was sent out with the draft, under the command of Colonel Daubeney and they landed about the same time as the regiment at Soutari, on the 21st of May, 1854.

He then began to reminisce about his fighting days in one of history's troubled times. By September they had landed on the plain of the Eupatoria, been supplied with ammunition and promptly put into action. Their duty to fight their way up the heights of Alma –

"A jolly hard task it was. Our clothing and accoutrements were heavy, we had strong cross belts, shakoos and each carried a muzzle loaded rifle. With us on the extreme right were the French, what rattling good fighters they were, keen as mustard, plucky and stickers.

Of course mind you, I say it without a single doubt, there was no soldier in the wide world to lick the English Tommy. On we chaps went at the word of command. The Russians, from their batteries, were sending shells and firing down from the heights with rifles onto the advancing battalions. I saw men tumble to the left of me, to the right of me. Our band chaps carried them off as they dropped. The duty of the untouched men was to take those heights."

"We crossed a river which took us up to our middles. Out on the other side, and on we went without a quiver. We were right in the zone of fire, you could hear the shriek of the shell, the rush and ping of the bullet. Although we felt nervous and whackery the fighting feeling came over us and we spared nothing to get at 'em. We worked up the heights and the ranks of the fallen were filled. Britons and Frenchmen went side by side right to the crest, and the Russians seeing that they were being overwhelmed, abandoned guns and positions and retreated into Sebastopol. A lot of arms and ammunition fell into our hands."

"Our next great fight was at Balaclava, where the English and the French were engaged. I did not take part in that battle being one of a picket party, but I saw it. It was a tremendous fight, and the plain was strewn with the dead and wounded. There were some blunders here. The charge of the Light Brigade, to recover the guns, was a madly brave thing. I saw men fall from their horses, and mad gallopers rushing about. There was a great and needless sacrifice of gallant life on that day. Seeing that I was only a spectator of the fight, I have little to say about it."

He then told the reporter of his next great battle, which took place in late October of that year, and involved a heroic charge by a small body of men in what he termed his "little Inkerman", and which was later incorporated in Kingslake's historical writings in the following manner - "Without firing a shot Colonel Daubeney, at the head of his 30 men of the 55th, had been all this while approaching the right flank of the great trunk column, and, perceiving, when near, that the head of the column was engaged with troops in its front, he resolved to attack its second battalion. That second battalion, as it happened, had been ordered the moment before to deploy to its right, and the evolution was beginning accordingly, when Colonel Daubeney sprang at its flank with the 30 men he was leading, and along with his people he not only wedged himself in between the second and third companies of the rival battalion, but tore his way on and on into the centre of the mass. There, at one time, the assailants and the assailed stood so closely locked together that their power to hurt one another was, during some instants, suspended.

"At length the men worked their way on. Some were wounded, some slain, and some taken prisoner, but the most of them still held their course, still went on forcing their way betwixt the howling ranks of the enemy. This singular charge did not end until Daubeney with the remains of his 'thirty', had cleaved a path through the battalion from flank to flank, and come out into open air on the east of the great trunk column. Besides Colonel Daubeney himself, there came out alive a number of men who had charged with him through the battalion, and amongst them were Thomas Leyland, Donald McIntosh, William Smith, Jeremiah Ready, John Stokes, James Ryan, John Prindiville, and William King."

In May 1906 war hero Thomas Leyland recalled his fighting days half a century before.

His battles and his son's are recorded on the memorial in Preston's Avenham Park.

Mr. Leyland then recounted how the effect of the charge had put the Russian battalion in a state of confusion, and prevented them from being let loose on a section of the broken French soldiery.

"The Russians were staggered; they thought we had more men than we had, and retreated. I felt, when fighting, that I could have smashed through a boiler. Soon after we came through we couldn't find our men. They had shifted. I was hit on the head with a fragment of a shell, and was taken to hospital".

"I recovered sufficiently to take part in the capture of the Redan. The forces, French and English, were well disposed for the grand attack. We lost a lot of men as we approached the Redan, for the Russians had a tremendous lot of batteries of all weights, and they bore the guns hard on us. But we went on and on, and, as you know, we captured the Redan, slaughtered a lot of Russians and captured a great number of prisoners. It was a great war, not without its privations and sufferings, but we forgot those in the glorious hour of victory."

Thomas Leyland was justly proud of his military career, and showed the reporter his Crimean Medal with bars for Alma, Inkerman and Sebastopol, as well as the Turkish War Medal and the long service medal for good conduct.

When peace was proclaimed he had a stint at Gibraltar, followed by spells in Cork, Dublin, Jersey and Portsmouth. When he left the 55th he joined the Shropshire Light Infantry and with them spent a number of years in the West Indies. Eventually returning to England, leaving the army and on doing so being granted a small pension.

In May, 1862 he had married the woman who sat opposite

War memorial in Avenham Park

him in the rocking chair. She was one of the fair lillies of Jersey and the couple had several children, two sons who survived to share their later years.

The youngest son, with whose family the Leyland's shared their Birchall Street home, had been through the Boer War with the North Lancashire Regiment and had two medals and at star to prove it. The ladies of the house were said to be very proud that both their warriors had earned the decorations of their country.

When the account of the reporter's visit appeared in the Preston Guardian, the headline read 'A Hero of the Crimea – an Historical Charge.'

In future, when I pass down Inkerman Street, I'll think of Thomas Leyland, its just a pity that the Sebastopol Inn is no longer with us because a visit to drink to his memory would have been appropriate.

Source:
'Preston Guardian' 12th May 1906

Chapter 15

HON. E.G. STANLEY

The Derby Memorial Statue

At the Preston Quarter Sessions in January, 1877 two youths named James Edward Dobson and James Paul Roberts, both residents of the town, appeared before the Magistrates charged with unlawfully and maliciously defacing the statue of the 14th Earl of Derby which stands in Preston's Miller Park.

In January 1877 the Derby memorial statue was daubed with blue oil paint.

A great deal of excitement had ensued when the Derby Memorial statue had been discovered following the action of the youths. The young men had entered the park after closing time and using a rope to scale the monument, had daubed it with blue oil paint. Garters had been painted on the legs of the statue, attempts had been made to paint a sash on the body of the monument and patches of paint had been smeared on the lower part of the face and figure.

The statue, paid for by public subscription as a sign of the respect the townsfolk of the

19th century felt for the late Earl and the House of Stanley, was at first thought to have been the object of some political activists.

As the court proceedings unfolded the two youths admitted their guilt and it soon became clear that their actions had been nothing more than a lark. They had been horrified by the reaction to their thoughtless prank and seemed heartily ashamed of what they had done.

The cleaning up operation had already commenced by the time the court sat and the difficulty of removing the oil paint from the marble statue was related to a packed court, which included many local trades people.

After much deliberation it was decided by the Magistrates that little good would come from sending the youths, who both had good character references and were from respectable families, to prison and it was agreed that provided the cost of cleaning the monument was met by them they may retain their liberty. By the end of the day certain guarantees were received from their families and they were allowed to walk free from the court. As he dismissed them, the chairman of the Magistrates reminded them that their actions had brought down on them a degree of public calumny which they would find hard to bear, and which only many years of honest industry and good character would enable them to efface.

The statue had been unveiled on Whit Tuesday, 1873 and had cost in the region of £2,500 towards which working men, by penny subscription, had contributed £346.15s.7d. It was reckoned that the unveiling ceremony took place before a crowd numbering close to 40,000.

Made of Sicilian Marble it stands 11 feet high and, in both features and general figure, it is said to be a very striking likeness of the nobleman it represents. The attitude is that of addressing the House of Lords: The Earl holds a scroll in his right hand, and on the same side below, there are three volumes – Homer's 'Iliad' etc. – in which he took a special interest. His robe of rank – taken off – rests upon the inner ends of the books.

The pedestal of the statue is of polished grey granite, 13ft. 6ins. high and it rests upon a base of grey and red granite, three feet in thickness. The statue itself weighs some six tons and the pedestal about forty.

On the front of the pedestal is the inscription, "Edward Geoffrey Stanley, 14th Earl of Derby, K.G. Born 29th March, 1799. Died 23rd October, 1869."

In the early years of the 20th century, as the local suffragettes movement gained momentum, the statue once again became the focus of public attention. The inhabitants of the Borough awoke one morning to discover that the honoured house of Derby had been insulted and brought low.

The Earl of Derby's statute had been tarred completely from head to foot and at the base of it was placed a placard which boldy emblazoned the slogan, 'Votes for Women'. News soon spread of the inglorious decoration of the famous politician and once again a clean

William Pitt, *Tory*, Dec. 7, 1783.
Henry Addington, *Tory*, March 21, 1801.
William Pitt, *Tory*, May 16, 1804.
Lord Grenville, *Whig*, Feb. 10, 1806.
Duke of Portland, *Tory*, March 31, 1780.
Spencer Perceval, *Tory*, Dec. 6, 1809.
Earl of Liverpool, *Tory*, June 16, 1812.
George Canning, *Tory*, April 30, 1827.
Viscount Goderich, *Tory*, Sept. 8, 1827.
Duke of Wellington, *Tory*, Jan. 26, 1828.
Earl Grey, *Whig*, Nov. 24, 1830.
Viscount Melbourne, *Whig*, July 18, 1834.
Sir Robert Peel, *Tory*, Dec. 26, 1834.
Viscount Melbourne, *Whig*, March 14, 1835.
Sir Robert Peel, *Tory*, Sept. 6, 1841.
Lord John Russell, *Whig*, July 6, 1846.
Earl of Derby, *Tory*, Feb. 28, 1852.
Earl of Aberdeen, *Peelite*, Dec. 28, 1852.
Viscount Palmerston, *Liberal*, Feb. 10, 1855.
Earl of Derby, *Conservative*, Feb. 25, 1858.
Viscount Palmerston, *Liberal*, June 18, 1858.
Earl Russell, *Liberal*, Nov. 6, 1865.
Earl of Derby, *Conservative*, July 6, 1866.
Benjamin Disraeli, *Conservative*, Feb. 27, 1868.
W. E. Gladstone, *Liberal*, Dec. 9, 1868.
Benjamin Disraeli, *Conservative*, Feb. 21, 1874.
W. E. Gladstone, *Liberal*, April 28, 1880.
Marquess of Salisbury, *Conservative*, June 24, 1885.
W. E. Gladstone, *Liberal*, Feb. 6, 1886.
Marquess of Salisbury, *Conservative*, Aug. 3, 1886.
W. E. Gladstone, *Liberal*, Aug. 18, 1892.
Earl of Rosebery, *Liberal*, March 3, 1894.
Marquess of Salisbury, *Conservative*, July 2, 1895.

19th-century Prime Ministers. The Stanley heir, rejected by the Preston electors, went on to become Prime Minister on three occasions.

up operation was launched to restore the elegant monument. The local suffragettes, including leading campaigner Mrs. Edith Rigby, were suspected of being responsible for the outrage, but the authorities failed to charge anyone with the crime.

The Derby family had strong links with Preston and in 1826 the future 14th Earl of Derby, the Hon. Edward Geoffrey Stanley, stood as a Whig candidate in the town's Parliamentary contest. He was an apparently popular choice from the four candidates of differing political persuasions and he was returned at the head of the poll, capturing 2,994 votes during the 15 days of voting.

Four years later he repeated his success with a similar number of votes and seemed set for a successful political career. Then, as Earl Grey sorted out his ministerial appointments he invited the M.P. for Preston to be Chief Secretary for Ireland. He duly accepted and as was the case in those days, the Honourable Gentleman had to appeal to the constituency once again for re-election.

A formality surely for the local politician. However, the rapidly emerging Radical Party had other ideas and all their efforts were concentrated on the challenge of their candidate, Henry Hunt.

A full blooded contest took place and as the campaign progressed the Hon. E.G. Stanley gradually became unpopular with the working classes. His troubles increased when he made a political address from the upper windows of the Bull Hotel in Church Street. He displeased the people by his speech, during which he stated that he wasn't going to be returned solely by the lower classes or those wearing fustion (coarse cotton twilled fabric). They booed and hissed him and the working classes turned against him.

Later, while going down Lune Street, he was set upon by a mob, back and front; and at the corner of Fleet Street he was thrown down and spat upon, being shamefully abused. A local shopkeeper came to his rescue, dragging him out of the gutter and into his shop. Hiding the M.P. in a closet he cleverly diverted the rioters in the wrong direction and solicited the aid of two plain clothes constables. The officers then accompanied the distraught politician back to the Bull Hotel and away from the unruly mob.

Considerable dodgery was said to have taken place at this election, but the Huntites claimed there had been as much irregularity on the Stanley side as there had been on their own.

The final poll revealed the defeat of the Hon. E.G. Stanley and the Radicals rejoiced in their triumph. While doing little damage to the political career or the political future of Edward Geoffrey Stanley, the election result did nothing to strengthen the town's ties with the Derby family.

He was soon back in parliament being elected for Windsor with a special arrangement being made with Sir Hussey Vivian who vacated his seat there.

In fact, politically, he went from strength to strength and on three occasions he was the Prime Minister of Great Britain. Firstly, in 1852 as Whig representative and then in 1858 and 1866 as a Conservative Premier. Indeed, the statue is a reminder of one of the 19th centuries most influential politicians.

The Derby family had periodically occupied Patten House, situated on the northern side of Church Street, between Derby Street and Pole Street, but after the election upset their visits became less frequent. While occupying the house, they had been known for their kindness to the poor and their presence was missed.

The premises forsaken by the Derby family were demolished in

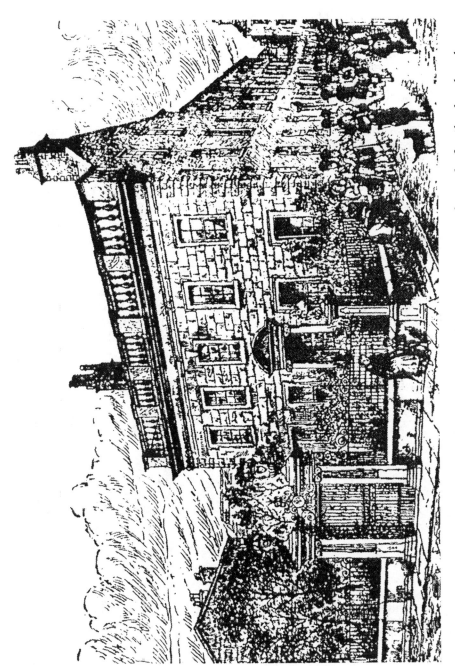

Patten House - when the Hon. E G Stanley was rejected by the Preston voters the Derby family abandoned their Church Street mansion – it was demolished in 1835.

1835. The house had been inherited by the Stanley family following the marriage in 1688 by Sir Thomas Stanley to Elizabeth, daughter of Thomas Patten, who was M.P. for Preston in that year.

By degrees, the Derby family withdrew from everything of popular or prominent character in and around the town that they had been associated with. In 1833 the horse races on Fulwood Moor, which they had patronised so generously, came to an end.

It took a considerable period for the wounds inflicted by the town's rebuff of the Stanley family in 1830 to be healed, but eventually they were.

One man who played a prominent role in the renewing of the Stanley family connection, was Frederick Arthur Stanley, the younger son of the man whose statue graces Miller Park. An illustrious Conservative politician he represented Preston in the House of Commons from July, 1865 to December 1868 when he was elected for North Lancashire. Recognised as a friend of Preston from his early days, the town's rulers acknowledged his contribution to the welfare of Preston by choosing him as Guild Mayor in 1902.

Coming just a few weeks after the Coronation of King Edward VII, the Guild was a lavish affair. The Earl of Derby showed that as the 20th century began the links between town and family were once again strong. This was emphasised by the conferring on him of the Honorary Freedom of the Borough. An honour also bestowed upon his son, Edward George Villiers, the seventeenth Earl of Derby, in 1937.

Sources:
    Hewitson's History of Preston
    'Preston Chronicle' January 1877
    'Preston Chronicle' July 1851
    'Preston Guardian' September 1902

The 16th Earl of Derby, Lord Mayor of Liverpool 1895, Guild Mayor of Preston 1902

Chapter 16

HENRY 'ORATOR' HUNT
Radical Party Member

In February, 1831 the Radical Party member representing Preston made his maiden speech in the House of Commons. For Henry 'Orator' Hunt it was the culmination of his greatest triumph. A place in the House having been gained at the expense of a Stanley heir and, indeed, a future Earl of Derby.

Twice before, in 1820 and again in August 1830, Henry Hunt had tasted defeat in Preston while contesting elections under the flag of the Corn Law agitator and reformer William Cobbett. The third time, in December 1830 he was returned in triumph, at an amazing election at which both sides were accused of fraudulent practice to obtain votes. Over 7,000 votes were recorded and it was claimed that a host of strangers had been brought to Preston for the purpose of tendering on behalf of Henry Hunt.

Initially his opponent, the Hon. E.G. Stanley, lodged a protest against the proceedings of the election. However, after objections by Henry Hunt the defeated candidate 'thought better of his intention of having the votes scrutinised' and withdrew his objection.

Certainly Mr. Stanley had strong grounds for his objection as two years later, when the first register of voters was made, there were only 6,291 people who possessed the right to vote by virtue of residence. This figure being arrived at after a period when the population of the town had significantly increased.

The final poll revealed 3,730 votes for Henry Hunt and he was

In a hot-blooded strife-rousing election Henry 'Orator' Hunt defeated the future Earl of Derby.

elected with a majority of 333. It had been 'a hot blooded strife-rousing affair', according to one historian and Hunt's victory was commemorated by the striking of a medal by his admirers in London. The silver memento given to each of the voters and paid for by national subscription was inscribed with the words, "One of the 3730 electors of Preston, 1830".

After the election numerous squibs were issued, one of which contained the following verses:

> O Preston, Preston, once so proud,
> Hast thou not now proclaimed aloud,
> In honour thou art lacking?
> To reject the noble Stanley's son,
> And let thy choice be fixed upon
> A Blackguard son of blacking!
>
> O Preston, Preston, shame to thee,
> Thou'st stampt thy name with infamy,
> Thy glory is departed;
> Thy honour in the dust is laid,
> A bye-word and a scoff thou'rt made,
> Of all that's noble-hearted.

On the 3rd of February 1831 the triumphant Hunt was escorted to Parliament at the head of a great procession of reformers and agitators.

Once in Parliament he attacked not only the government plan of reform, but openly criticised his friend Cobbett and other associates. His aim was to form a new party, with himself as leader, and he campaigned for many drastic and radical changes.

It didn't take long for Parliament to grow tired of his constant disputation and excess of words and always supersensitive of criticism, he stammered, blustered and finally sank into gloomy silence. In October of the same year he neglected the House and toured the manufacturing towns of Lancashire, Cheshire, Yorkshire and Staffordshire. At these places he found food for his wounded vanity in a series of mass meetings, where he swayed thousands with his hectic and stentorian oratory.

He was never at ease more than when he was in the limelight and in 1819 he had been involved in the Peterloo Massacre. In fact, some regarded him as the 'hero' of that particular occurrence. Whilst speaking to the people of Manchester he had witnessed the famous

Involved in the Peterloo Massacre was Preston's future M.P.

incident with the troops and the 80,000 protestors which resulted in about a dozen deaths and the injury of several hundred others. It was claimed in some sources that Hunt's silly vanity in poking fun at the yeomanry had provoked the attack upon the crowd assembled.

Following the incident Hunt and others were arrested and confined several days in Lancaster Castle. They were eventually bailed out awaiting trial and made their way back to Manchester by road, through Preston, Blackburn and Bolton. Frenzied multitudes of people acclaimed them, waving banners and shouting, "Hunt for ever" and "Down with the tyrants".

Hunt continually stood up, doffed his white hat and bowed gracefully to the crowds, who were like incense to his self-love for which his whole heart seemed to beat.

At the subsequent trial at York Assizes, he conducted his own defence. When proceedings finished he was found guilty of unlawful assembly and sentenced to two years imprisonment. Whilst in prison he wrote his own memoirs up to the year 1812. The volume described as 'wordy, turgid and wearisome' was said to have 'glory be to Henry Hunt' as its sole theme.

Born on November 6th, 1773 he was the son of a prosperous Wiltshire farmer and he never tired of recalling that at one time he had the best flock of Southdown sheep in the country.

As a young man his zeal for sport led him to his career as a radical orator. His sporting activities often resulted in quarrels with neighbours and on one occasion imprisonment, which enabled him to mix with Reformers. Subsequently he was to become the most popular hero of the early 19th century Reformers.

Men and women flocked to hear him and the cry 'Hunt and Liberty', became a common phrase. He preached a message of hope and he had the ability to make his audience believe they were on the winning side. His white hat and tall figure became symbols of a happier future.

In 1806, he took a prominent part in the elections for Bristol, and for Wiltshire. Six years later he was an unsuccessful candidate at Bristol, complaining afterwards that bribery and illegal violence had cost him the seat.

It was to this background that Hunt swayed the people of Preston to believe in his ideals and ambitions. He had, for a time, many loyal supporters in the town and numbered amongst them were Joseph Livesey and the temperance disciples. His visits to the town were very infrequent, however, and the general feeling began to prevail that he only visited the town when he needed the votes. As his Parliamentary career developed, the inhabitants of the town began to see him as a man with a domineering vanity and ingratitude.

The Government Reform Act of 1832 meant an early return to the polling booths as a new Parliament required election. Foolishly Henry Hunt believed that he still had the support of Preston's inhabitants and as a result did little campaigning in the town.

Five candidates contested the town's two vacancies and amongst them was another member of the Stanley family that Hunt had triumphed over in the previous election. On this occasion, the voters deserted the Radical candidate and the Hon. H.T. Stanley gained revenge for his brother's defeat. Along with Mr. P. Hesketh-Fleetwood (founder of Fleetwood town and harbour) he earned the right to represent the inhabitants of the town in the new constitution.

Henry Hunt took his defeat badly and, financially in dire straits, he was forced to travel for orders as a manufacturer of blacking. Whilst so engaged, he was seized with paralysis and died on the 13th of February, 1835, at Alresford in Hampshire.

It was a cruel end to the life of a man of enormous vanity and self esteem. Unquestionably he did, during his years of political activiity, goad the Government of the period along the path of representative equality in Parliament. In Preston he is best remembered as the man who made it fashionable in Lancashire for Radicals to wear white hats.

Henry Hunt – Born November, 1773 – Died February 1835.

Postscript:
On his visits to the town, Henry Hunt often rode on a white horse named 'Bob' and with his white hat he made a spectacular impression. When the horse died it was buried in the back garden of a house near Ormskirk Road. A few years later the horse bones were dug up and sold as souvenirs - a gruesome reminder of the glorious orator.

Sources:
Hardwick History of Parliament
'Manchester Guardian' February 1935 (Centenary Article)
'Preston Herald ' September 1945
Hewitson's History of Preston

Chapter 17

RICHARD ARKWRIGHT

Industry was Hanging by a Thread

The night before Christmas Eve in 1732 was a significant occasion, not only in the history of Preston, but also in that of the nation. It was a wet and windy evening in the old town as a family that already struggled to feed twelve little ones, prepared for the arrival of another.

The little working class home that stood somewhere near the present day 'Stanley Buildings' in Lancaster Road, had its doors and windows shuddering in the wind and rain cascading down its window panes, as hope once again sprang eternal. In an upstairs room there soon arrived another hungry mouth to feed.

It was a boy and the Arkwright family welcomed its thirteenth child into their world of poverty. Little could they have known that night the child they cradled in their arms was to become one of the founders of the Industrial Revolution.

There was little time for childhood in those dark, despairing days, and by the time he was eleven Richard Arkwright was apprenticed to the trade of barber and wig maker. In all it took seven years to learn this eighteenth century trade which included primitive dentistry, the extracting of bad teeth and bleeding of the sick in the hope that good blood would replace bad. From the latter practice, signifying blood and bandages, the familiar red and white pole of the barber was derived.

After serving his time he went to Bolton to set up business on his own. Once there he befriended the daughter of local schoolmaster Robert Holt. The couple were married and in 1755 she gave birth to his only son, Richard.

Locally, Richard Arkwright became well known and was very ambitious and hardworking, and the development of a hair-dye was credited to his expertise. Constantly in need of human hair for wig manufacture, he often toured the district.

Sadly his first wife died within a few years and it was on one of his traveller's errands that he met the woman who became his second wife. He was visiting Leigh when he made the acquaintance of a daughter of a respectable inhabitant, named Biggins.

Recognised as a man with a certain 'genius for mechanics' he was always visiting households where spinning and weaving took place. He was aware of the efforts of men to invent substitutes for the old fashioned handwheel, and the likely profits to be made by the man who could make improvements in the ordinary process of spinning by hand.

Arkwright was a frequent visitor to Leigh, where his father-in-law resided, and in that district there lived a man called Thomas Highs who was developing an idea of spinning rollers, and had engaged a local watchmaker, John Kay, to construct a model for him. Not in particularly good circumstances, Highs permitted his scheme to hang fire making little progress with it.

The next significant occurrence took place in 1767 when Kay, who had left Leigh to reside in Warrington, met up with Arkwright in one of the town's taverns. The outcome of their meeting was the renting of a room in Preston, in the house of the headmaster of the Grammar School, at the bottom of Stoneygate.

Arkwright and Kay demanded privacy and security to their lodgings and they set up their spinning machine in the first floor room. Occasionally, strange noises were heard coming from the building and the two men were soon the subject of curious conjecture.

The noises were said to be like 'the devil tuning his bagpipes' and there were those who would have broken into the premises to reveal what was going on. At the time, however, the town was deeply engrossed in the hot blooded parliamentary election of 1768, and Arkwright and Kay were able to complete their spinning machine without disturbance.

Sir Richard Arkwright – poverty in youth made him proud in success.

Arkwright House - in 1768, in a first-floor room, Richard Arkwright developed his spinning frame.

Shortly afterwards in July, 1769, Arkwright was granted a patent for his spinning frame, which had two vital features others did not. Firstly, the correct spacing of the spinning rollers and secondly, the weighting of the rollers to nip the fibres tightly.

Prior to this patent, James Hargreaves, a joiner from Stanhill, had introduced a 'Jenny' which spun eight threads but only spun soft weft. This machine had been regarded as superior to the device that Thomas Highs of Leigh had invented with Kay.

Initially Arkwright had his machines powered by horses on a site in Nottingham, where also Hargreaves had fled after trouble with the Luddite factions, who had destroyed his machinery in the riots at Blackburn.

In 1770 with the financial backing to go with his technical know-how, Arkwright established himself on a site at Cromford in Derbyshire, using water powered machinery. There he laid down the principles of the factory system, with its carefully arranged flow of work and strict supervision.

It is generally acknowledged that James Hargreaves, Richard Arkwright and Samuel Crompton, who invented the 'Spinning Mule' in 1779, revolutionised the cotton industry.

By 1775 the mills at Nottingham and Cromford were both profitable, and Arkwright was able to build further mills in Lancashire, Derbyshire and the adjacent counties. He became a very rich man on account of his patent licence fees and in 1785 he opposed Parliament's decision not to extend his patents, but was unsuccessful. In fact Arkwright had been accused of invention stealing and both Highs and Kay gave evidence of a confused nature. The reality of the matter was that it had been better for progress' sake that Arkwright had developed Highs' unfinished ideas into something practicable.

His poverty in youth made him proud in success and he climbed the social ladder. He built a magnificent mansion 'Willersley Castle' near Cromford and in 1787, while the High Sheriff of Derbyshire, he received a knighthood from King George III.

When he died on the 3rd of August 1792, aged 59, he left behind an industrial empire that was a tribute to his endeavours. His remains were interred at Cromford and he was said to have left property worth £500,000. He was not a genius; but had much tact and insight and knew what the times required. If he could not invent much himself, he knew how to utilise those who could. A remarkable man indeed, old Arkwright, not much culture but plenty of shrewdness.

Postscript:
In October, 1991, the 'Daily Telegraph' announced the impending closure of Masson Mill, on the River Derwent, at Matlock Bath in Derbyshire, once the flagship of Sir Richard Arkwright. From 1785, for over two centuries, production had never stopped at the world's oldest continuously working mill. In Arkwright's time, the millhands had toiled for 13 hours a day in the hot, dusty mill. If they arrived after the six o'clock bell stopped ringing, they were locked out and lost a

Sources:
  Hewitson's History of Preston
  Biography of Richard Arkwright. 'Preston Guardian' May 1894

Chapter 18

HORROCKS FAMILY

Rise of the Cotton Trade

In May, 1988 the world famous textile firm Horrockses announced a complete relocation of their business, to new premises on the outskirts of Preston on the town's Red Scar Industrial Estate. Ironically the new site was once the home of the booming Courtaulds textile empire.

The announcement also meant the end of operations at their old fashioned Centenary Mill in New Hall Lane, Preston. The company had in almost two centuries operated from many sites in the town and the Centenary Mill, built in 1891 to celebrate the firm's 100th birthday, was the company's biggest operating base from 1962, when the town's cotton industry suffered its biggest blow with the closure of the firm's huge works in nearby Stanley Street.

The business was started in 1791 when the young quarryman, John Horrocks, arrived in the town and rented a small building in Turks Head Court, where he produced yarn for handloom weavers. Keen to expand his business interest he went into partnership with Thomas Greaves and Richard Newsham who were able to obtain the necessary capital.

Agreements signed, he was able to begin the development of his cotton empire. Firstly, the 'Yellow Factory' was erected at the southeastern end of Church Street. Then five years later 'Moss Factory' appeared, followed quickly by the 'Frenchwood Factories' in 1797 and 1798, 'Canal Factory' in 1799 and, in 1802, a mill in Dale Street.

Besides these buildings, spread around the town, he also built a number of handloom sheds, with cottages adjoining, in the New Hall Lane area. The 'Yellow Factory' was the first of a great mass of buildings that became known as the 'Yard Works'.

By then a prosperous business man and in partnership with his brother Samuel, he turned his attention to the political scene. Encouraged by his friends who disliked the 'Derby influence' on parliamentary matters he became a candidate in the 1796 election.

Narrowly defeated, his political aspirations were undeterred and in 1802, he succeeded in becoming the parliamentary representative of Preston, when his election was unopposed.

Tragically his new-found status was short lived as he died in March, 1804, at the tender age of 36. The ailment under which he sank

JOHN HORROCKS
founder 1791

John Horrocks arrived in Preston in 1791 to start a business that would last for almost two centuries.

Born in 1768 – died March 1804. In a remarkable 13-year period he left an indelible mark on the town.

The company founded by John Horrocks became the largest textile manufacturers in all England.

The 'Yellow Factory' was erected at the south-eastern end of Church Street. Note the date stone 1791.

was inflammation of the lungs and his death occurred in London, in which place he was not only attending to his parliamentary duties, but to the extensive commercial operations of the firm of which he was the head.

Born at Edgworth, near Bolton, in 1768 he had, during a remarkable 13 year period, left an indelible mark on the town and its people. His development of the cotton trade in Preston had been quite astonishing and his premature death was a great shock to all. He was buried in Penwortham churchyard in a grave covered by a massive flat stone slab, surrounded by high strong iron railings. Among the many mourners were his two sons Peter and John, aged 13 and 10 respectively.

Following the sudden death of John Horrocks, his brother and business partner Samuel succeeded him as the Member of Parliament for Preston. Samuel Horrocks was something of a rough diamond and made no pretence to be either a scholar or a gentleman. Like his brother, he had a somewhat limited education and this showed in the coarseness of his manner. Sadly, he was constantly badgered about his inability to express his political view either by speech or in writing.

Despite being a shrewd businessman and a master cotton spinner, he was often criticised as incompetent in his role as a Member of Parliament. He very rarely spoke in the House of Commons and became known as the silent member. One tale that has survived the years is that a penny sheet was circulated in the town containing a speech made by him in the House – in fact it was a blank sheet of paper.

Nonetheless, he remained a Member of Parliament until 1826 having success at a number of elections. He also spent 30 years as a Borough Magistrate and as a member of the Corporation of Preston. In fact, he was Mayor of Preston in the year 1802/3, succeeding the Guild Mayor, Nicholas Grimshaw.

The parents of the Horrocks brothers lived to see their advancement and the maternal heart beat proudly in 1802 when on a visit to Preston, their mother saw one son walk down the aisle of the Parish Church as Mayor, at the head of the Corporation and the other son walk down the aisle as the Member of Parliament for the Borough.

In July, 1823, Samuel Horrocks survived a murder attempt on him by cotton operative Andrew Ryding. After attending the Parish Church Samuel was making a Sunday morning visit to his business partner, Thomas Miller, when he was attacked from behind, being struck twice on the head with an iron cleaver.

At his subsequent trial the 22-year-old assailant, a member of the Preston Union, said that he had become enraged by the oppressive attitude of the cotton baron; claiming that Horrocks had been responsible for the falling of wage levels in Preston and the victimization of strike leaders on their return to work.

In 1833 the then Alderman Horrocks retired from public life and to mark his retirement the members of the Town Council presented him with a silver gilt box, containing a resolution praising his public character and service.

A father of eight, seven daughters and a son, Samuel lived at Lark Hill House (later to become Lark Hill Convent) which he had built in the early part of the nineteenth century.

His wife, Alice, had died in 1820 and he departed this life in March, 1842 aged 76, dying at his Lark Hill home. He was buried in St. George's churchyard in the same grave as his wife.

At the time of his death his only son Samuel Horrocks was the Guild Mayor of Preston. Educated at Eton, he was groomed to take an active part in the business of the great cotton firm founded by his uncle.

In 1827 he had married the second daughter of Thomas Miller, who had been associated with Horrockses from the early days, when he had been brought from Bolton to assist by John Horrocks.

During the early years of their marriage they lived at no. 9 Winckley Square, next door to the Winckley Club. After the death of his father the couple took up residence at Lark Hill House and it was from there that he carried out his Guild Mayor duties.

The 1842 Guild was held at a difficult time for the town. Preston had become a large and densely populated place geared up for cotton manufacture. Despite the recent Lune Street riot, in which, as Mayor, he had played a central role, the majority of the Corporation was in favour of holding the celebration and the age-old event was successfully held.

Less than four years after the Guild he was dead, dying in February 1846 at the age of 49. His funeral procession was a most impressive affair with all the pomp and ceremony befitting a man of his position. With the cotton empire silent, close to 200 attendants – two abreast – walked behind the cortege as it made its way to St. Paul's Church. He was buried in St. Paul's churchyard near the north east corner of the church.

His departure in some ways signalled the end of an era although the empire created by his uncle rolled on.

*A cracked gravestone in St. George's churchyard marks the last
resting place of Samuel Horrocks, Senior.*

Indeed, it was only by 1870 that the industry in the town seems
to have been at its peak. Then the number of mills and sheds in Preston
numbered 76.

The decline in the cotton industry started shortly after and by
1880 trade was in a dull and retrograde state. In a disturbing decade,
twenty cotton mill fires occurred and many strikes took place, as
relations between masters and operatives were far from cordial.

Lack of orders necessitated closure of mills, there being much
fluctuation in the home and foreign trade. Competition became
intense in the foreign markets and it made itself felt as the 19th century
drew to a close.

The outbreak of the First World War sounded the death knell
to the considerable Chinese and Indian trade. Cotton mills had been
erected in India and protective tariffs imposed but the Japanese, with
their cheap labour, captured the Chinese markets, as well as making
significant inroads into the Indian trade. It wasn't long after the
cessation of hostilities that almost all the mills in Preston serving the
Indian and Chinese markets were forced to close down.

Indeed, by the time of the Second World War, the local trade was confined to the finer cloths and specialised fabrics. The 32 remaining mills at that time continuing through skilful labour and the use of silk and rayon with the cotton.

The present day cotton trade in the town bears little resemblance to that planted in the very bones of our local ancestors by John Horrocks, those two centuries ago.

Postscript:

The move to Red Scar turned out to be only a short-lived one. In March 1990 the closure of the last Horrockses factory in the town was announced with the loss of 150 jobs.

Sources:
'Preston Herald'
18.4.1941 and
15.11.1940
Dobson's Parliamentary History of the Borough
Hewitson's History of Preston
Hardwick's History of Preston

The greatest name in cotton proclaimed this 1952 Preston Guild advertisement.

Chapter 19

REV. CARUS WILSON
Church Builder of the Borough

On the 21st of October, 1823 the Vicar of Preston, the Reverend Roger Carus Wilson, laid the foundation stone of St. Paul's Church in Preston. Deposited in the cavity of the stone was a glass jar which contained a Preston Chronicle printed upon parchment, a bronze Guild Medal and some gold, silver and copper coins of the past and present reigns.

The church was built on land formerly ringed with trees and known as 'The Park' and the final cost of the building was just over £6,500.

This church and its sister church, St. Peter's, whose foundation stone was laid in Guild Week 1822, were among the many built nationally to commemorate the Battle of Waterloo. The costs being met from a parliamentary grant which totalled £1 million.

Roger Carus Wilson became Vicar of Preston in March 1817 and his incumbency is chiefly remembered for the great increase of churches within the old borough boundaries during his term at the helm. The living of the Parish Church was secured for him by his father, a former M.P. for Cockermouth, who purchased the right for £1,500 from Sir Philip de Hoghton.

Twenty-five years old at the start of his incumbency, he was a very energetic man with an impressive and delightful style of delivery, which earned him the affection and esteem of his congregation.

With the growth of the cotton industry and the influx of families into the town the new churches attracted healthy congregations. This convinced the vicar that further churches were required to cater for the spiritual needs of the town's residents.

He thus embarked on a building programme that further transformed the surroundings of the neighbourhoods. Firstly, the faithful of the Bow Lane area were blessed with construction of Christ Church, which was consecrated in October 1836 by the Bishop of Chester, Dr. Sumner, a future Archbishop of Canterbury.

Next to benefit were the people of the New Hall Lane area of the town, who watched with interest as the Norman style of architecture took shape and became St. Mary's Church. Built on land formerly

St Paul's Church – the Rev. Carus Wilson laid the
foundation stone in October 1823. The church
building is now home to the tuneful melodies
of Red Rose Radio.

St Peter's Church,
Preston, built in Guild
year 1822 at a cost of
£7,000.

known as 'Jackson's Garden', the church was consecrated in June, 1838.

As construction work was coming to an end at St. Mary's, attention was focused on a piece of land in Lancaster Road, close to the junction with Moor Lane. There a Norman style edifice was developing into St. Thomas's Church, and in June, 1839 the consecration took place.

The cost of St. Thomas's was £5,600 and this expense along with those for the construction of St. Mary's and Christ Church were met from a fund of £50,000 bequeathed by a Miss C.E. Hindman for the purpose of church building.

The money enabled the Rev. Carus Wilson to also purchase the former 'Primitive Episcopal Church' in Avenham Lane, which had come on hard times. A Church of England offer of £1,000 in 1838 secured the premises and the church of St. James' was consecrated in June, 1841.

Besides these expansions of the established church within the borough boundaries the vicar also extended his interest to the Ashton area. As a result, for an outlay of just £2,000 another Norman style construction was credited to his name, with the building of St. Andrew's church, on what is now known as Blackpool Road.

A busy and vibrant minister he was totally immersed in the churches he had been instrumental in establishing. Therefore in December, 1839 the town was completely stunned by the news that came from his home in Winckley Square.

An announcement that he had died very suddenly on Sunday afternoon, the 15th of December, aged 47, was met with shocked disbelief. Apparently during the previous week the vicar had been much exposed to the cold and inclement weather and, on the previous afternoon, had gone to bed with what appeared to be a slight cold.

Anxious to preach on the Sunday morning he had to be persuaded by his wife to stay at home and rest. He had seemed much improved at that time but by mid afternoon, after a few more hours sleep he awoke feeling worse. The arrival of a neighbour who perceived that his condition was serious, led to the summoning of medical and spiritual aid. However, before either could arrive to give assistance, the Vicar of Preston had passed away.

The consolation for the parishioners, who mourned his loss, came in the realization that during his twenty-two years as Vicar of Preston, he had developed the Church of England so much that he left behind a legacy of church construction the town could be proud of.

Christ Church in Bow Lane. Nowadays what remains is used as a conference centre and chapel.

St Mary's Church (off New Hall Lane) – consecrated in June, 1838 and still a place of worship.

99

Ironically, if the Rev. Carus Wilson should now look down from his heavenly abode he would see much change to his dedicated exertions. Of the churches accredited to his spiritual endeavours, only St. Mary's and St. Andrew's remain solely as places of worship.

St. Paul's is now home to the tuneful melodies of Red Rose Radio, who took over a dilapidated building in 1981. St. Peter's, another impressive architectural example, is now an Arts Centre and an integral part of the Central Lancashire University concourse. St. Thomas's remains a beautiful landmark in the North Road area, despite its closure as a place of worship in October, 1983. Its future now seems secure with its recent adoption as an Age Concern Centre. Christ Church had its original building closed in 1970, and a dual purpose building was constructed on the site. This doubles as a conference room and as the Chapel of Christ the King.

The church of St. James which dominated Avenham Lane with its magnificent tower is no longer with us. Closed in 1983, it was eventually demolished with porous stonework and dry rot abounding.

In remembrance of this remarkable vicar there is in Preston Parish Church, on the south wall of the Lady Chapel, an elaborate memorial. Inscribed with the words, 'Erected to his memory by those who loved him living and mourned him dead', it shows in relief the five new churches erected through his exertions within the Borough of Preston. His body lies buried under a simple block tomb slab at the head of the Nave aisle.

Rev. Carus Wilson – Born 1792 – Died December, 1839.

Sources:
Hewitsons – Churches and Chapels
Records of Preston Parish Church
History of the Borough of Preston
'Preston Guardian' December, 1889

Chapter 20

FRANCES, LADY SHELLEY

A Society Lady

In the year 1787, in a large house on the south side of Fishergate, Preston, between Cannon Street and the New Cock Yard, there was born Frances Winckley. She was the daughter of Thomas Winckley, a large owner of property, after whom both Winckley Square and Winckley Street were named. He was a direct descendant of the de Winkelmondeleys who , in the Saxon times, settled in a corner between the Ribble and the Calder. Her mother was the widow of Major Hesketh, who died young from a severe wound received during the American War of Independence.

At the time of Frances Winckley's birth her father had begun to grow disenchanted with Preston, which had to that time been regarded as the winter residence of the nobility. The erection of cotton factories in and around Preston was the main source of his disgust and things came to a head shortly afterwards. Making his usual early morning visit to the fishmongers, to select the fish for dinner, he found that he had been forestalled by a Mr. Horrocks, a cotton spinner. The fact that the finest turbot had been denied him was too much for his dignity.

Pronouncing Preston no longer a fit place for a gentleman to live, he immediately rented a villa situated about four miles outside Liverpool - then a rising, but still small, town. The house stood on a beautiful hill, overlooking the Mersey and surrounded by lovely woods. It was an idyllic place. As things transpired Thomas Winckley did not long survive this removal, dying when his daughter was barely six years old.

During her short life he had played many pranks, including on one occasion taking her from her bed, in the middle of the night and transporting her in a coach, with four black horses, his servants in tawny orange liveries, to Blackpool, his Brighton of the North.

He had practiced as an attorney in Preston but spent much of his time in London, where he led a bachelor life. The charms of his conversation and wit delighted his contemporaries and his wife was subject to and dare note oppose his whims.

After her father's death, Frances Winckley was taken to London to live in the house of the aged Lord Stair. A couple of years later she was sent to a small child's school in Twickenham and there she made great progress in french and music.

An ambitious, but somewhat delicate child, she caused her mother anxiety by developing symptoms of consumption. At once she was transferred to Clifton, under the care of a Dr. Beddoes, a man well known for his successful treatment of such patients. His idea of an infallible cure was to place

Lady Shelley - born Frances Winckley, daughter of Thomas Winckley.

patients in rooms above cowhouses. The belief was that the breath of the cows ascending through gaps in the flooring and inhaled by the sufferer, would prove a remedial treatment.

Whatever the merits, or otherwise, of her treatment it proved successful. In the next few growing years she had to survive much upheaval in her life. Not least the untimely loss of her mother, which led to her living at Winwick with her guardian; at Knowsley as guest of Lord Derby, and then with her half brother, Sir Thomas Hesketh and his charming wife at Rufford Hall.

At the age of 15, under the instructions of Lady Derby, she was sent as a pupil to London to prepare for a place in society as befitted an heiress. Two years later she was ready to mix in the upper circles and the Heskeths took a town house in London for the season. The Heskeths mixed with the best in society and numbered amongst their acquaintances members of the Royal Family. As a result Frances Winckley met her future husband, Sir John Shelley, a descendant of the poet Percy Bysshe Shelley. Her mature suitor was described as a distinguished looking man with a handsome face. Over the next couple of years their friendship developed.

On the 4th day of June, 1807 the couple were married at St. George's in Hanover Square, London. By this union the Winckley property in Preston, Catterall, Brockholes, Balderstone and Fulwood went into the Shelley family. Their marriage produced six children, four sons and two daughters.

Lady Shelley became a great society lady meeting many royal personages, as well as such people as Sir Walter Scott, Lord Broughton and the Duke of Wellington. A woman of energy and determination, she was keenly interested in church and religious matters.

Her husband died in 1852, aged 81 and Lady Shelley later removed to the Isle of Wight. She had a residence built in the East Cowes area and from 1867 she spent most of her time there. While residing there Queen Victoria made her acquaintance and on each royal visit to the island, the Queen always made a point of visiting Lady Shelley at her Maresfield Lodge home. She died at her Isle of Wight home in February, 1873 at the age of 85.

The story of Frances Winckley can be followed in the 'Diary of Frances, Lady Shelley', which was published many years after her death. It gives an insight into high society life in the first half of the nineteenth century.

Lady Shelley – Born 1787 – Died February 1873.

Sources:
Diary of Lady Shelley
Hewitson's History of Preston

DIARY OF FRANCES LADY SHELLEY

CHAPTER I

I WAS born at Preston, in Lancashire, in 1787. My father, Thomas Winckley, of Preston, was a direct descendant of the de Winkelmondeleys who, in Saxon times, settled in a corner between the Ribble and the Calder. My mother, who was the daughter of Hew Dalrymple, descended from a kinsman of President Lord Stair, who carried the Union with England. She had previously been married to Major Hesketh, who died young from a severe wound received in the American War of Independence. By her first husband she had one son, afterwards Sir Thomas Hesketh, and six daughters. My mother had a charming personality and was perfectly beautiful, with the celebrated "Dalrymple brow," so well known in Scotland. She was, of course, very proud of her Scottish descent. She was not judicious in the management of her "lambkin" (as she used to call me), a name which I resented, as I felt that I had much more of the lion than the lamb in my disposition. I disliked her impetuous caressing, and early learnt to allow myself, as a favour to *her*, to be kissed; and not, as is usual with most children, to receive a caress as the reward of good conduct and maternal affection. Although my mother spoiled me; there was a strong sympathy between us, and I liked to sit on her knee and listen to the old Scottish Jacobite ballads, and the sweet poetry of Burns.

Chapter 21

ANGELA BRAZIL

Worked, Played, Loved, Prayed, Passed On

One weekday morning in 1873 the ten year old Amy Brazil left her home in West Cliff Terrace, Preston clutching the hand of her four-year-old sister, Angela. Their destination was the nearby select Ladies school run by the two refined and elegant sisters, Miss Knowles and Miss Eleanor.

Amy was one of their regular flock and keen to increase the number of pupils the sisters had arranged for the young Angela to make a start in her education. The school however, had no proper arrangements for tiny children, with all the pupils being taught in one large room.

Angela was received with favour, but within half an hour the sisters were regretting her admission. She was innocent of sedate discipline and not even 'Mary's Little Lamb' could have upset the school more as she 'made the children laugh and play'. Fun was her aim that morning and the younger sister, Miss Eleanor, was eventually instructed to cope with the spirited youngster.

She kindly took her on her knee and began to reason with her in a gentle tone. The affectionate Miss Brazil clasped her arms tightly round her tutor's neck and looked long and deep into her eyes. The soothing words of reason made little impression because, as the patient Miss Eleanor spoke, a tiny pair of hands, with wicked little fingers, were busy removing hairpins from her head. Suddenly, Miss Eleanor's coil of long hair came down and a smothered titter from the class informed her of what had happened.

Angela Brazil - her epitaph was 'Worked, Played, Prayed, Passed On'.

The young Miss Brazil was banished from the comfort of her tutor's knee onto the cold reality of a hard wooden form. An unsuccessful knitting lesson, a tearful Amy and an outraged Miss Eleanor brought an abrupt end to Angela Brazil's first morning at school. With hairpins back in place, Miss Eleanor marched the girls back to the Brazil household and to a solemn interview with their mother.

It meant temporarily a suspension in the educational plans for Angela Brazil, a girl who, in later life, was to become one of the most prolific writers of her time. Her first morning at school was recalled when she penned her much acclaimed autobiography, 'My Own Schooldays'. This book being written after her many successful novels with titles such as, 'Schoolgirl Kitty', 'The Princess of the School', 'The Fortunes of Philippa', and 'The New Girl at St. Chad's'. The stories recall the days when schools were crammed with girls who battled for honour, relished team spirit, adored the fifth formers and dreamed of success at sport. Indeed, for any schoolgirl of the early 20th century a treasured Christmas gift was the latest Angela Brazil novel.

Angela Brazil had been born in Preston on St. Andrew's Day, 30th November, 1868 to proud parents Angelica and Clarence Brazil. Her father, of Irish descent, was a Cotton Broker and her mother, born in Rio de Janeiro, was a British subject of Scottish Highland origins.

The family that fate dropped Angela Brazil into in those Victorian days, was already furnished with two brothers and a sister. She arrived after a gap of 6½ years and Amy believed she was the urgent answer to her many and earnest prayers for a baby sister.

When Angela was almost five, the family lifted up their roots and left Preston to live at Egremont, a suburb on the Cheshire side of the estuary of the River Mersey. They removed there for a number of years before living for spells in Bolton and Manchester.

The next significant chapter of her life began after her father's death, when in search of sunshine she, Amy and their mother, spent several winters wandering in Italy and Sicily. Later winters were spent in Palestine, Egypt and other foreign places and the summer base of the family became a country cottage in Wales at Llanbedr. It was a disused farmhouse, which had been built long ago from the ruins of an ancient Cistercian monastery.

It was there, living an idyllic country life, that Angela Brazil began her writing. The first story that she sent to the publishers, Messrs. Blackie, was 'The Fortunes of Philippa', which was an almost exact rendering of her mother's early years.

In her Welsh setting she loved to be surrounded by local school children and they inspired her writing, as she caught the atmosphere and saw matters from their angle of vision. They often had picnics in the hills, supper parties by a bonfire, cricket matches, paper chases, theatricals and various other fun. As a result all the characters in her books became every bit as real as were her many young friends in actual life. In an evening, by a log fire, or during the daytime by a stream, she penned chapters by the score.

The result was international acclaim and thousands of teenage devotees eager for the next helping of schoolgirl literature. By the end close on fifty titles had reached the bookshelves. As her autobiography suggests, she lived a full and varied life and millions of her books were sold at home and on foreign shores. She died in March 1947, and her epitaph which brings her autobiography to a close reads thus :

'Worked,
Played,
Loved,
Prayed,
Passed on'

On hearing the news of her death, someone in Messrs. Blackie suggested it wouldn't be long before they received a manuscript titled 'The School at the Pearly Gates'.

Angela Brazil – Born 30th November 1868 – Died March 1947.

Sources:
  My Own Schooldays – Autobiography
  Children's Writers Publication

Chapter 22

NICHOLAS ARROWSMITH

Shadow of the Workhouse

Down the centuries the common logic of the people was 'when everything else fails, there is the workhouse'. As the name suggests it was a place where work might be obtained for the relief of the able-bodied poor. It was also the place of refuge for the sick, infirm and elderly who were provided for by sums publicly levied.

The plans for providing employment and relief were established by an Act of Parliament passed in 1601. Throughout the seventeenth century Preston's less fortunate were provided for by private bequests. Any 'foreigner' or 'stranger' who arrived in the town faced being put out if he should become burdensome after a three month stay.

Only in the latter part of that century did Preston make strides to provide a workhouse and this stood on the north side of Avenham Lane, at the corner of Bolton's Court in the Syke Hill area. Under the control of a governor the residents were set to work from six o'clock in the morning until six o'clock at night. They worked at the woollen trade and the yarn produced was for the making of clothes and stockings.

The thought was that "It was better to have them working under supervision, than to be left to wander the streets begging." Those who appeared to suffer from idleness faced the wrath of the Corporation and even a term in the old House of Correction.

In 1782 a law titled 'Gilbert's Act' was introduced with the intention of unifying neighbouring parishes to establish a 'poor house'. The old Avenham Lane workhouse was abandoned and its place was taken by a white edifice, which was erected at the southern end of what was then called Preston Moor.

Down the decades fear, dread and revulsion became the by-words associated with the Deepdale establishment. Like many of its national contemparies it earned an unenviable reputation and various reports and inspections only added to its abhorrence.

The inmates of the Deepdale Workhouse had the following weekly menu:

Breakfasts - Bread, and a sufficient quantity of porridge, made of one gallon of good new milk to two gallons of pure and clean water, with a proper quantity of oatmeal or flour and salt. When milk is scarce, beer may be used in stead of it.

Suppers - Water porridge, made of good, sound and sweet oatmeal, with sweetened beer, or with buttermilk, when plentiful as a change.

Dinners - Sundays, boiled beef, Thursdays, fried bacon, with a sufficient quantity of potatoes of other vegetables, and salt, each day; Mondays, soup made from the broth, Wednesdays, hash or stew, Fridays, bacon dripping with a sufficient quantity of bread, potatoes or other vegetables, and salt each day; Tuesdays and Saturdays, lobscouse, made from a sufficient quantity of the coarser pieces of beef, and potatoes, with pepper and salt. Everyone to have as much as is required, but no victuals whatever to be taken by the paupers out of the eating-rooms, after the meal is finished.

The rules for the Deepdale establishment drawn up in June 1827:

WORKHOUSE RULES

-No pauper to enter the house or to be discharged therefrom without an order from one of the Overseers or from the Select Vestry.

-That the Poor in the House be classed both in the day, working, and sleeping rooms, as far as may be practicable, as follows, viz:-

1.- Old and Young Men, without Families.

2.- Old and Young Women, without Families.

3.- Married Men, their Wives, & Families.

4.- Widowers, with Children.

5.- Widows and unmarried women, with children.

6.- Women during the month of confinement.

7.- Infants at nurse, and children too young for school.

8.- Boys, if possible, in two classes, according to their ages.

9.- Girls the same.

- No Person in the House to go out of it on any pretence whatsoever, without leave from the Governor or Governess.

- The Males not to enter the apartments of the Females, nor the Females those of the Males.

- All the Paupers above ten years of age, to go to bed at nine o'clock at night, from Lady-day to Michaelmas, and eight o'clock the remainder of the year. The bell to be rung to denote those times. The children under ten years of age to go to bed at an earlier hour.

- All the Poor who are able, to attend the prayers; to come clean to the table; and to sit decently at their meals; not to talk nor leave their places till thanks be returned.

The Borough of Preston, }
in the County of Lancaster. }

AT a special session, holden at the Town Hall, in and for the said borough, we, EDWARD ROBERT TRAVERS and NICHOLAS GRIMSHAW, Esquires, two of his Majesty's Justices of the Peace for the said Borough, do approve of and allow these Rules and Regulations.

Dated this twenty-sixth day of June, one thousand eight hundred and twenty-seven.

E. R. TRAVERS,
NIC. GRIMSHAW

In March, 1867 the 'Morning Star' newspaper carried an article that had appeared in the 'British Medical Journal'. It concerned an Inspector's recent visit to the Preston Workhouse and the report delivered to the guardians.

The report was scathing in its criticism and it described the charitable house as old, ill-managed and unsuitable in every respect. Ventilation was said to be a phenomenon unknown, and the wards were dark, gloomy and unhealthy.

The patients, both infirm and those suffering from serious contagious diseases, slept two or even three in one bed. No closets or conveniences were available, save for a few buckets distributed through the wards.

Some inmates were said to be without clothing and in particular shoes and stockings. While for the sick, there was no waterpoof sheeting or air cushions for their comfort.

There was an absence of any attempt at cleanliness and the wards were swarming with vermin.

In conclusion, the inspector stated that his visit had been one of the most distressing and repulsive that he had ever made to a work-house.

Without doubt, the report had uncovered some of the inadequacies of the local institution, but when it was discussed at local authority level, the conclusion was that it was a 'highly coloured' document.

Prior to this article, plans were already afoot to build a new workhouse to supplant all of the existing workhouses within the Preston Union. At the time, besides the Deepdale workhouse, there were others in Ribchester, Woodplumpton, Bamber Bridge and Penwortham, making up the Preston Union, in line with The Poor Law Act of 1834.

Eventually, in December, 1868 on the north side of Watling Street Road, Fulwood the new building was opened. With an imposing external structure, a wide sweeping facade and a clock tower above the main door, it was to become the centre of a residential quarter – a mark of poverty among the moderately well to do.

School and workrooms, dining hall and chapel made it the paupers' palace, which, with the later addition of hospital wings, was able to accommodate up to 1,500 people.

Stone-breaking and land-tilling were the labours of the able-bodied men, the partially disabled spent their time picking oakum. The able-bodied women did the washing and housework, boys were taught tailoring, shoemaking or baking and the girls learnt to knit, sew and clean.

The imposing but somewhat forbidding clock tower on the Fulwood Workhouse

Conditions were much improved in the new workhouse, although inmates were still subjected to iron disciplines and strict rules and regulations. It was still the last place of refuge and none wished to linger there longer than was necessary. The shadow of the workhouse still loomed large over those driven to hard times.

An article in the 'Preston Guardian' at the beginning of October, 1885 under the title, 'Sad Reverse of Fortune' reflected the fear that lurked in everyone's heart. It concerned an old Preston family called Arrowsmith and, in particular, Nicholas Arrowsmith, who during his lifetime had experienced extraordinary vicissitudes.

In the early part of the nineteenth century his father, Richard Arrowsmith, had carried on an extensive business as a woollen trader and importer of Irish linens and provisions. One of the town's leading tradesmen, he had premises at 32 Market Place, near the Castle Hotel.

In 1825, in association with Messrs. Lowe, Roskell and Hudson, he had started a banking business. With various partners and mergers, Richard Arrowsmith continued in that field until being succeeded by his eldest son, Robert. Their dealings had been chiefly with the Catholic community and great confidence was placed in them, as down the years they had weathered several commercial crises, when larger concerns had succumbed.

The bank of Messrs. Roskell, Arrowsmith and Kendall was therefore entrusted with nearly all the Catholic charitable funds of the town. Unfortunately in May, 1867 financial problems engulfed this bank, as it had so many others, and payments were suspended with liabilities of over £70,000. In the end the partners, Mrs. Roskell, a widow from Liverpool, Robert Arrowsmith and John Kendall, gave up everything to their creditors.

Robert Arrowsmith was completely shattered by the events and died soon after the affairs of the bank had been wound up. The failure was attributed to a run on the bank and to the losses occasioned by a large spinning mill at Walton.

Nicholas Arrowsmith, the younger son of the founder Richard Arrowsmith, was never associated with the bank, nonetheless he was said to have lost a considerable fortune when it went down. This coupled with bad speculations in sheep farming in Australia, led to him being driven to seek shelter in the workhouse.

Misfortune had piled on misfortune and he was forced to adapt to his new circumstances. Not an easy thing for one accustomed to the comforts of comparative wealth. He endured life in the workhouse until the end of September, 1885 when he had an apoplectic seizure which terminated fatally a couple of days later. During his dying hours the 67-year-old was attended by two local priests who administered religious consolation.

Postscript:
The Fulwood Workhouse building still lends its imposing presence to the local scene. Once home for over a thousand people, the building became the Civic Hostel in 1948 and, in 1971 Preston Corporation sold the premises to the Lancashire Health Authority. Used for a while as a home for the elderly, the premises nowadays are used as the headquarters of the Preston Health Authority.

Sources:
  'Preston Guardian' Oct. 3rd 1885
  Hewitson's History of Preston
  Whittle's History of Preston
  'Preston Guardian' Workhouse Report Mar. 9th, 1867.

Chapter 23

EDWIN HENRY BOOTH
'To Thine Own Self Be True'

In the year 1859 Edwin Henry Booth returned to Preston, where he had spent part of his youth apprenticed to the grocery trade, and purchased premises in the Market Place which he opened as 'The Tea Establishment'. It was the latest venture for a young man who, against great adversity, had managed to develop a business that would become a flourishing family firm.

Born in Bury, Lancashire in 1828 Edwin Henry Booth was the son of surgeon Thomas Booth who had a large practice in that town. His mother, one of twelve children, was from London where she was previously married, as a teenager, to a gentleman engaged in trade with Russia. Alas, he lost his fortune in the unstable Europe of the time and he died soon after, leaving his wife with a son and daughter.

Edwin Henry Booth's mother left the children by her previous marriage in the care of her father and the future looked bright for young Edwin. Unfortunately, soon after his birth his father was killed in a street accident and his mother was once again left unprovided for.

Ill luck seemed to follow the woman and a third marriage, this time to a gentleman with grown up children, was to lead to further tribulations. The new-found stepfather turned out to be a drunkard and life for young Edwin and his dear mother was one of 'hell upon earth'. Often the stepson was forced to flee from the man's presence and take up shelter with charitable neighbours.

Eventually he was driven away from home in Rochdale and after tramping his way to Bolton sought employment as an errand lad. Few eleven-year-olds were more enthusiastic than young Edwin and for three shillings a week he would deliver parcels until midnight and then walk the several miles to his lodgings, with a family his mother had been acquainted with.

Edwin Booth returned to Preston in 1859

The errand lad became a draper's assistant and then got a situation in a grocers shop. He asked little for his hard work and loyalty, save for a few shillings or a place of lodging. So it was with the grocery job for which he received bed and board on the premises as remuneration. His master at that time was a very religious man and on Sunday young Edwin attended Chapel morning and evening, on each occasion the master would give him a small coin to place in the collection. On the other six days work began at eight o'clock in the morning and was rarely finished before eleven o'clock at night.

His closest companion at the time was a destitute orphan girl, the general servant of the establishment. When work was over, the pair would sit together in the cellar kitchen with Edwin reading to her the hymns of Wesley.

Also employed by the grocer was an elder apprentice who quite unjustly accused Edwin of robbing his master to pay for some articles of clothing. The couple of shillings involved had in fact been given to Edwin by a former acquaintance of his mother. When his master confronted him, Edwin viewed the matter with utter disgust informing his employer of his character and stating - "I never took a thing in my whole life which was not my own, and whatever my troubles, or whatever my poverty may be, I never shall".

Edwin broke down in grief to think he should be so unjustly treated and one evening soon after he had an up and down fight with the other apprentice. Although he came off much the worse, he had been able to vent his anger. Dusting himself down and placing his cap on his head he then left the place.

After gaining shelter for the night with a friend, and with three shillings from a dear old lady who had always shown him great kindness, he set off next morning on the road to Preston. By nightfall that Saturday he had reached the town and was knocking on the door of his half sister's dwelling place.

First thing on Monday morning Edwin was at the Market Place seeking employment. Willing hands were always welcome and a grocer by the name of Threlfalls agreed to employ him on condition of obtaining a good reference. His former master refused to reply to his new master's correspondence and as a result Edwin was forced to return to that place to obtain a reference and collect the few clothes that he had left behind.

When his former employer saw Edwin he told him that his greatest wish was that he should return and that he would give him a salary of £18 per annum. Edwin declined the offer and on his return to Preston his new employer informed him that he would match the salary offered.

Aware of his poor education, Edwin resolved to do something about it and every night after business hours he took his copy book, arithmetic and grammar up to his attic room and worked away till going on for midnight. Often he would also rise at five in the morning and study for three hours before the day's business commenced. In all the teenage apprentice lived a disciplined existence and twice on Sunday he visited church.

During this period he learned that his stepfather had died in Liverpool in distressing circumstances and consequently his mother was left without a home. As a result he was obliged to contribute a portion of his eighteen pounds per year to his mother's upkeep.

His employer had ambitions to extend his business into Blackpool, which had become linked to the expanding railway system, and the intention was to train Edwin to manage the premises. But when Edwin's apprenticeship was over his employer did not have the resources to carry out his plans.

Although very poor, Edwin realised the potential at the seaside resort and despite his financial shortcomings he was able to impress an hotelier in Blackpool sufficiently to get him to convert a barn in the main thoroughfare into a shop. Edwin agreed to pay the man fifteen pounds per annum for the premises and after obtaining eighty pounds of goods on trust from his former employer he was in business. Soon he was doing a brisk trade with the leading hotels and principal consumers and after three months of working almost night and day he had made a profit of fifty pounds.

Although business peaked in the summer months he still kept a fair sale in the winter time. Soon the barn shop was being pulled down to be replaced by purpose built premises.

Always to the front in his thoughts was his poor mother without a fixed home and dependant on his assistance. To resolve the situation he took a nice house in the suburbs of the town, not far from his place of business and his mother moved in to manage the place.

Not long afterwards he was to meet the young lady who would become his wife, Susannah Phillips, the daughter of a corn miller from Colne, who was staying with her mother at the house of a lady of his acquaintance. His business took up much of his time but his thoughts often strayed to the girl of his dreams. Following proceedings of protocol his romance eventually blossomed and visits to her home in Colne and expressions of his honourable intentions paid dividends.

116

The couple were married in October, 1853 in Colne and after the wedding and honeymoon, he took his bride to his newly built small detached house in the seaside resort. In the period before the marriage Edwin had succeeded in finding a comfortable home for his mother so that the young couple were able to begin married life alone.

In time the pair became the devoted parents of a daughter, a beautiful, precocious darling. The couple were anxious to exploit their youthful energy and Edwin resolved to extend his business to Chorley where he opened a shop in 1855, and where they went to live. Chorley proved successful but they felt that it was not the place they wished to settle.

Edwin had developed an affection for Preston during his apprenticeship and in consequence he resolved that he would buy the premises in the Market Place. His only regret was that his former employer was still there and he was wary of doing anything that would give the appearance of opposition. As a result he took up only one branch of his trade, that of tea merchant.

His premises, right in the centre of town, were amidst the leading tradesmen who remembered him as the poor apprentice. It was not a happy homecoming but a troubled time. An underlying resentment existed and the other traders did much to undermine his credit. They made recourse to many falsehoods in an attempt to prevent his progress. In response he took a firm stand and depended upon his capabilities as a business man. Within a few years his enemies had dispersed and he was rewarded with easily the largest share of the grocery trade in the town. The purchase of two shops in Fishergate in 1867 for £3,000 being testimony to his success. In the years that followed business boomed and Lytham and Blackburn branches were added to the enterprise.

Despite their business success the family were not without their domestic tribulations. Shortly after they had been blessed with a son the daughter they had doted on died at just three years of age. To add to their woes, both Susannah's parents died within a short space of time and Edwin's mother then passed away during a tragic period for their household.

As time went on and the couple became settled in Preston they were blessed with three more daughters and four sons. Sadly one of the little fellows died aged 2½ years, the victim of diptheria. He was buried besides his little sister and the distraught parents consoled themselves with the hope that they might one day see their dear faces again in Heaven.

Young Edwin had been apprenticed to the Threlfall's establishment in Preston Market Place.

As each of his four sons came of age, Edwin Henry Booth introduced them into his grocery trade. It was not, however, to the liking of them all and the second son preferred to take up the wholesale tea trade in London, while the third son eventually became a doctor at St. Annes. The eldest, John and the youngest, Tim concentrated their efforts in furthering the family concern. Both becoming directors in due course with John taking on a great deal of the burden by becoming a junior partner in 1880 and helping to guide the business towards becoming a Limited company in 1896.

The family had a happy home life residing firstly at 10 Bank Parade and then at Avenham Tower, an attractive Italian style villa situated at the corner of Bank Parade and overlooking Avenham Park.

Edwin Booth was a tender hearted man and he always thought of the less fortunate, working actively with many local organisations in caring for deprived and neglected children. With the assistance of friends he was able to form an Orphan Aid Society for the little ones who trod the path that he had been forced to follow. In the role of treasurer of the Harris Orphanage, he was able to oversee the developments that occurred after Edmund Robert Harris left a considerable portion of his fortune to the orphans of the town. His achievements were many, not least of them being his rescue of the local Electrical

Supply Company, when financial disaster loomed and, when Preston Dock was opened, he chartered a ship and brought in a cargo of tea and groceries to mark the occasion.

During his final years he wrote his autobiography which he called 'Shadow and Sheen'. It was published as the life story of Alec Gordon, which was the pseudonym for Edwin Henry Booth. In it he had advice for poor boys, urging them to cultivate a feeling of self respect and self reliance, trusting only in their own individual efforts. The work which chronicled his life ended with the verse 'To Thine Own Self Be True'.

> By thine own soul's law, learn to live,
> And if man thwart thee, take no heed;
> And if men hate thee take no care;
> Sing thou thy song, and do thy deed,
> Hope thou thy hope, and pray thy prayer,
> And claim no crown thy will not give,
> Nor bays they grudge thee for thy hair.
>
> Keep thou thy soul-sworn steadfast oath,
> And to thy heart be true thy heart;
> What thy soul teachest learn to know,
> And play out thine appointed part;
> And thou shalt reap as thou shall sow,
> Nor help nor hindered in thy growth,
> To thy full stature thou shalt grow.
>
> Fix on the future's goal thy face,
> And let thy feet be lured to stray
> Nowhere, but be swift to run,
> And nowhere tarry by the way,
> Until at last the end is won,
> And thou mayest look back from thy place,
> And see thy long day's journey done.

The affable grocer, known for his honest trading and sheer hard work, died in January, 1899 at his Avenham Tower home. At the time he was just one week short of his seventy-first year. The report of his death stated that he had been a generous and kindly man, willing to support any deserving cause brought to his attention.

Avenham Tower, home of Edwin Henry Booth during his latter years.

Postscript:
As time passed the Fishergate premises were developed into a spacious modern up-to-date building with an upper floor cafe, capable of accommodating over two hundred people. Generations of Preston people took a break from their shopping to enjoy afternoon tea or a morning coffee amidst the splendour of the Booth's Cafe. It was therefore much regretted when the town centre store closed for business in September, 1988.

Despite that closure, the family-run business still flourishes and stores remain on the outskirts of the town in Fulwood and Ashton as well as at other locations throughout Lancashire, Cumbria and Cheshire.

Edwin Henry Booth – Born January 1828 – Died January 1899.

Sources:
Autobiography 'Shadow and Sheen'
'Preston Guardian' January 1899